Essay Writing for
High School Students

Alexander L. Terego

THOMSON

PETERSON'S

Australia • Canada • Mexico • Singapore • Spain • United Kingdom • United States

About Thomson Peterson's

Thomson Peterson's (www.petersons.com) is a leading provider of education information and advice, with books and online resources focusing on education search, test preparation, and financial aid. Its Web site offers searchable databases and interactive tools for contacting educational institutions, online practice tests and instruction, and planning tools for securing financial aid. Thomson Peterson's serves 110 million education consumers annually.

For more information, contact Thomson Peterson's, 2000 Lenox Drive, Lawrenceville, NJ 08648; 800-338-3282; or find us on the World Wide Web at www.petersons.com/about.

ISBN 0-7689-2063-9

Printed in Canada

10 9 8 7 6 5 4 3 2 1   07 06 05

First Edition

Contents

Acknowledgments

First and foremost, I wish to recognize the invaluable contributions of my wife, Nancy. Nothing happens until an idea is suggested, and she gets the credit not only for suggesting the idea for this book, but also insisting that it be written. My thanks also go to Jane Phelan, who has edited all my work and whose suggestions are unfailingly helpful. In the early days of the project, Nancy Clarke and Lynn Reifert of the Study Center in Venice, Florida, aided me ably and immeasurably.

Once I had finished the first draft of the book, I was helped by three English teachers and 105 of their grade 11 and grade 12 students at Booker High School and Pineview High School in Sarasota, Florida, and Lakewood Ranch High School in Manatee County, also on Florida's west coast. I am indebted to David Bustard, an attorney at Williams Parker in Sarasota for facilitating this.

Mrs. Cathy Lane, Mrs. Linda Janoff, and Mrs. Coquina Homer deserve a special vote of thanks, as do their students—each of whom read the book, filled out a questionnaire, and wrote a competitive essay. These teachers' suggestions became part of the final copy; without them, I am sure the book would be less useful. The three winning essays submitted by their students appear in Appendix A.

I am particularly grateful for Mrs. Lane's suggestion that a Teacher's Guide be developed as a companion to the book and for her help in its development. The Teacher's Guide is intended to help teachers help their students to think and write. More information about the Teacher's Guide can be obtained at www.petersons.com/authors/terego.

I am also indebted to Mrs. Pat Bishop, then Supervisor of Secondary Language Arts for Hillsborough County Public Schools in Tampa, Florida. Despite her heavy responsibilities, Mrs. Bishop took the time to review this book and make many helpful contributions.

My heartfelt thanks go out also to Jane Sander for her constancy and encouragement. I would be remiss in not acknowledging Martin Levin and Helen Wan for their invaluable legal advice.

Finally, I thank Terri Moore, Executive Editor at Thomson Peterson's. She helped enormously by giving shape to my book, and she was a constant help in shepherding me through the process from first draft to publication.

Introduction

Imagine for a moment that a high school student, who is proficient in grammar, sentence construction, spelling, punctuation, and thesis identification skills, is asked to compose a 250- to 350-word essay on the following topic: *Explain why it is important to learn to write a competent essay.* The student might well answer by beginning with a solid thesis statement, or point of view, and continue by proving this thesis true, as in the following example.

essay

Several factors are driving the essay back to the top of the list of academic skills in which high school students must demonstrate proficiency. These factors are academic, professional, and personal in nature. After a generation or more of neglect, society has recognized the need to instill in students more than just an aptitude for guessing the right answers to multiple-choice questions. Educational professionals are realizing that colleges and future employers need to know if their candidates can think and express themselves by the end of a high school education; and writing is the best measure of that.

The popular examinations taken toward the end of high school now include an essay, required or optional, that provides significant information for evaluation of a student's abilities and potential. If this were not reason enough to begin studying essay composition immediately, colleges require an essay as part of the application process. Furthermore, a state university with about 6,000 freshman openings will typically receive 30,000 applications. In other words, only 1 in 5 will be accepted. The best private schools accept even fewer: about 1 in 10. According to the Summit Educational Group, "The race to gain entry into the nation's best colleges and universities has never been more competitive." The educational correspondent of the *New York Times* recently wrote that "Much of the decision making about a student's admission comes down to whether the admissions officer likes the student's essay."

Of course, there are other reasons to learn the art of essay writing that have nothing to do with getting into the college of your choice. The art of persuasion—rhetoric as the ancient Greeks called it—is best developed through debating and writing, and both are life skills with evident and long-lasting benefits in business and professional circles. Essay writing, in particular, develops the creative, critical, and analytical thinking of its practitioner. However, as a teenager just starting out in life on my own, my favorite reason for learning to write is monetary. College graduates earn, on average, one million dollars more over their careers than do high school graduates. If you do not find these reasons persuasive, may I suggest writing an essay on why essay skills are irrelevant?

How would a student make so effective a journey from the prompt to the thesis statement and from the thesis statement to the points that offer its proof? That question is actually the starting point for this book. The answer is at the heart of the method on which the book is based.

Why should you pay attention to what I say? Well, many years ago, as an 11-year-old with few prospects, I was fortunate enough to pass an examination that entitled me to go to a special school. The emphasis of that school was on academic achievement. The expectations were high, as were the standards. The key advantage of this school was that the teachers, who were members of the Salesian Order of Roman Catholic priests, not only demanded that we achieve high standards, but also gave us the tools to exceed. The most rewarding of these tools is the essay. My teachers knew that education is largely a process of self-discovery and that the essay is the best way to examine ourselves by examining our attitude toward a subject. The essay has served me very well, and I hope it does as well for you.

I went on to teach students how to pass examinations to gain entrance to Oxford and Cambridge Universities, using the essay techniques I had learned. I have had plenty of experience since then, and I have refined and improved those techniques.

I worked with more than 100 students in grades 11 and 12, after finishing a first draft of the book. Of these students, 98 percent found the book either very helpful or somewhat helpful, and 80 percent said they would buy the book and recommend it to a friend. I asked the students many other questions about the method and techniques in the book, and 79 percent felt these were very helpful. I invited the students' comments and was very pleased by the response. Here are just a few:

> "The book completely changed the way I think about writing an essay. It developed the way I think about things in general."
>
> James George Carolan, Pineview, grade 12

> "This collection of useful ideas for transmitting your personality and identity in an essay is very beneficial. This book helps me organize my thoughts by thinking contextually and visually. The diagram approach is very helpful."
>
> Hannah Kirsch, Pineview, grade 11

> "The amount of detail in this book is perfect. It's hard for an academic book to keep kids interested, but this one does. It's not just theory, it's useful."
>
> Joshua Sun, Booker, grade 12

> "The most important part of writing is thinking about it first. I never considered that before. Now I do. Thanks."
>
> Kate Atkinson, Booker, grade 12

About the Author

 After graduating from the universities of Manchester and London, Alexander Terego spent seven years preparing students for the Oxford and Cambridge entrance examinations. The essay was the main method used both for teaching and examination.

Mr. Terego then changed careers and spent the next three decades in the computer business, first in Europe and then in the United States. During this time, he developed and refined his methods for teaching thinking and problem solving. He calls this approach *Thinking Around the Box*™. He has taught these methods to high school students, graduate students, and business people.

CHAPTER ONE

Understanding Essay Writing

The subtitle of this book could easily have been *"Thinking Your Way Toward a Good Essay."* The real message of this book centers on thinking—thinking in a whole new way.

Some people who reviewed this book prior to publication suggested that, in explaining the principles and practices I have developed on how to write a good essay, I am expecting a little too much from today's average high school student. I disagree. I spent many years teaching at the high school level, and I believe that the essence of teaching is to expect *more* from students. It works on the athletic field, in the pool, and in the gym—why not in the classroom?

A near synonym for thinking, or perhaps an analogy for thinking, is *exploring*. Exploration is at the heart of the method I am teaching in this book. This method advises that the best way to form an opinion about something, such as an essay topic, is first to explore what you already know about the subject. Students know more than they think they know. A great deal of information is already stored in their memories. However, this information has to be teased and provoked to come to the forefront, to the conscious part of our minds. The good news is that there are ways to do this; you will read more about them in later chapters. That same process also reveals where the gaps in our knowledge are. In the course of reading this book, you will learn how to explore your mind for what you know about a subject and to examine the subject in order to discover more about it. You will then learn how to fuse or combine the two into a point of view and how to write a coherent essay that discloses what you have discovered.

Writing an essay according to this method can be compared to the famous thought experiments that led Albert Einstein to some of the greatest insights in history. In 1905, it was impossible for a young clerk in a Swiss patent office to construct the machinery that he would need to watch the activities of a beam of light or subatomic particles. Even if he had had the funds, the technology was not available to ride along as a beam of light whizzed by at 186,000 miles per second. It still isn't. In Einstein's time, physicists could not peer into the inner workings of the atom either.

His only option was to use his mind to explore the problem he was trying to solve by simulating what it would be like to ride a beam of light or watch as tiny particles swirled around inside their tiny universe. Instead of building castles in his mind, he built physics experiments inside his head. That is what discovering your point of view is like. It is a thought experiment—building castles in your mind. Go ahead, explore yourself, your mind, your personality. It is a very worthwhile exercise. You're not just writing essays, you are discovering who you really are.

If you are asked to explore a topic and write an essay about your point of view on issues raised by that topic, or prompt, the best way to do this is by using your brain to create thought experiments. The good news is that your brain is up to the challenge. Warning—it takes **lots of practice!**

Don't be like the first two quarry workers in medieval England who were asked what they were doing and answered "Cutting stones." Be like the third worker who answered "Why, sir, I'm building a cathedral."

If you, the high school student, pay close attention to this book, you *will* learn to write a good essay, possibly a really good essay. In the process, you will also learn something invaluable about yourself: namely, what you believe in.

The first mistake in writing an essay is to assume that the subject of the essay is the topic that the examiners have selected. If the examiners ask you, for example, to write an essay about a person who has influenced you, you should understand at once that the true subject of the essay is *you,* not the person who influenced you. Even if you are writing about the hazards of pollution or smoking, make no mistake: *you* are the subject of the essay.

People who read what you have written *will* know something about you after they have finished. What they know about you is entirely up to you. Like a baseball or softball pitcher, you control the immediate situation; the results—good, bad, or indifferent—are, as with a pitcher, entirely a product of your efforts.

THE KEYS

It really pays first to learn how to think your way toward discovering your point of view on a given subject and second to learn how to disclose, or share, what you have discovered. Here are the two main keys to essay writing that you should understand at the outset:

- **The First Key:** Composing an essay is an exercise in *discovering your point of view* about a subject or topic by using your imagination and thinking things through in an organized way.
- **The Second Key:** Composing an essay means *disclosing or sharing your point of view* in an organized and clear way.

By looking—in ways that you will learn later—at questions posed by examiners, you will discover what you believe about the matter in question. By observing the rules of writing, you will learn how to communicate those ideas convincingly.

For example, until someone asks you which person has been a great influence on your life, you probably never gave it much thought. By thinking about that question in a disciplined and structured way, however, you can uncover your genuine point of view, and discover one more aspect of yourself in the process. It makes perfect sense that only if you have thought an issue through will you be in a position to disclose what you have discovered. Otherwise, what you write is not authentic and will be revealed to your reader as such.

By first looking carefully at the essay topic, and then writing about it in your true voice, you permit the reader of your essay to get to know who you are. As you will discover, that is the goal of any essay.

This is what I call **writing with a purpose.** It helps you discover and refine your beliefs about all sorts of issues, large and small. Writing gives shape to who you are. Just as exercise builds your body, writing builds your personality.

A famous Prime Minister of Great Britain called Disraeli once said "The best way to become acquainted with a subject is to write . . . about it." Notice he did not say that the best way to become acquainted with a subject is to read about it or talk about it or think about it. Reading about a subject and talking and thinking about it are, of course, necessary parts of discovery; **but writing gives your reading a purpose.**

Just like a sponge soaks up water, reading soaks up information. Just like a sponge, your brain can become super-saturated and some of the facts and ideas need to be used or squeezed out and shared with others. Writing is the best way to refine all the knowledge you have gained into a personal philosophy that makes sense: first to you, and then to others. If the subject you are writing about is yourself—and it is—then it certainly makes sense to learn how to write a good essay.

At the time of the American Revolution, Doctor Samuel Johnson said "What is written without effort is in general read without pleasure." Your job is to make sure that the person who reads your essay gets pleasure from your work.

This book is designed to teach all the skills necessary—with the exception of penmanship—for writing a competent essay. The principles are the same for the timed essay that is part of the SAT and ACT Assessment and for the college application essay, whose only time constraint is the deadline imposed by the college.

Michel de Montaigne, a contemporary of Shakespeare, created the essay genre in sixteenth-century France. He said then, and it still holds true today, that "Essay writing gives reading a purpose and portrays a true image of the writer, as long as the essay is well argued and thoughtful." Think of essay writing as being like a mirror: an honest reflection of who you are.

Make no mistake about it, writing thoughtful, well-argued prose is a skill that is in demand not only by institutes of higher learning, but also increasingly in our complex, competitive, and sophisticated workplaces, where original thinking and communication skills are at a premium. Developing such a skill will be well worth your while.

A GOOD TIME TO LEARN

Developmental psychologists have demonstrated that adolescents, in particular, are capable of learning to be better thinkers; so it's good to be a teen. This is not surprising, since the human brain is *the* most complex entity in the universe. It is capable of astonishing feats and is at its most flexible and absorbent when the owner of this majestic machine—you—is still young. Learning to write a good essay should be a simple task for such an organism, and it is. Think of this book as just one small chapter in the "User Manual for Your Brain."

With ownership of such a magnificent machine as a brain comes responsibility. You have a duty to use it with care, deploy its mighty capabilities responsibly, and nurture it all of your life; not just for your own benefit, but for others too.

The amazing nature and capabilities of our brains goes a long way toward clarifying why we find answering right or wrong multiple-choice questions—at any age—a tedious, repetitive task for a mind whose nature it is to soar. Because of the mind's predictable response to this sort of challenge, the multiple-choice quiz alone has never been a fair measure of the person. At best, it is merely a predictor of a future ability to absorb and regurgitate facts. The multiple-choice quiz basically evaluates the left side of your brain and its rote memorization skills.

Mastery of algebra, history, or Spanish displays just one of our skills; the ability to learn and memorize what others have already discovered. The person—or these days more likely the computer—that judges and grades this skill is judging the test-taker objectively and learning very little about the person taking the test. The essay, on the other hand, allows for a subjective judgment to be made. Fortunately, as this book shows, this can be used to the essayist's advantage.

We Americans have now realized what many Europeans never forgot—learning to write well is, at its core, a creative, right-brained endeavor. Consequently, the reader of an essay is observing the essayist display knowledge of his or her *self* and how he or she relates to the world. The examiner of an essay can therefore expect to "hear" the person as they plead their case. In short, the essay is a valid surrogate for the applicant, a substitute for an interview.

This book will show you how to evoke a positive response in the College Admissions Director's mind or in the mind of the person judging your SAT or ACT Assessment essay. You *can* get the reader to say "That's good," or "That's interesting," even though you have no idea who that person is, what he or she looks like, how he or she thinks, and what he or she believes. You can do this even though the *Wall Street Journal* tells us that the SAT and ACT Assessment judges may read as many as 15 essays per hour.

By the way, the "canned" essay, the one that is written ahead of time in the hope that, with a little tweaking, it can be used to answer any essay prompt, will stand out like a sore thumb. There's no substitute for a glimpse of the real you.

In Short

1. The subject of the essay is you.

2. Writing gives reading a purpose.

3. Think your way to discovering your point of view.

4. Disclose that point of view to your reader.

5. Your essay will reveal whether you have truly discovered a point of view.

6. Your essay is your representative. Make sure it is authentic.

Thinking Around the Box™

A teacher hands your essay back to you with an instruction: "Be more original, John." The same teacher hands another student's essay back with the instruction: "Be more creative, Jane. Use your imagination."

You two bewildered students look at one another and shrug, as if to say "How? No one ever taught us how to be original or creative."

If the teacher had instead demanded more care in spelling, then little further explanation by the teacher would have been necessary. Creativity and originality, however, are more difficult to learn than grammar or spelling, since they are abstract concepts, and—note this well—the results are not necessarily right or wrong, good or bad.

Essay composition, however, *demands* that you demonstrate originality and creativity, as well as technical proficiency as a writer. This book will show you how you can master all three.

Let's begin by stating a principle fact you should know. An essay can be described as having three aspects: **style, substance,** and **type.**

Style is simply *how* you write. Your style will be judged by how well you follow the rules that govern English grammar, syntax, punctuation, sentence and paragraph building, and spelling. These rules all have to be learned; they are as fundamental to writing as multiplication tables are to arithmetic. There is no avoiding this, and the sooner you begin refreshing your memory the better. Some of these rules are reviewed in Chapter 7.

Substance is *what* you write about in your essay. In other words, *substance is the content of your essay*. Think of it as the message you want to convey to your reader and the arguments (logic and reason) you use to prove and convey that message. Developing a message and delivering it in the form of an essay is an exercise in originality and creativity as well as organization. Readers who grade the SAT and ACT Assessment essays will decide whether the message is clearly focused, well-developed, and well-supported. Anyone who reads your essay, including college admissions directors who read them online, will respond to the creativity and originality they express.

Type refers to the *kind* of essay. There are two types, informative and persuasive, and they are addressed in Chapter 5.

The good news is that originality and creativity, along with organization and the rules of style, can be learned. I have chosen to begin by showing you how you can learn specific ways of thinking about essay topics—or anything else for that matter. Don't be put off by their names. They are Contextual Thinking, Critical Thinking, and Creative Thinking. They are all part of *Thinking Around the Box*™.

CONTEXTUAL THINKING

I hope you noticed that a few paragraphs back, I said that essays can be described as having three aspects: style, substance, and type. That's a good example of how NOT to think in context.

Let me explain. Most of us tend to look at things, places, and people in the following way: once we see them, we immediately begin breaking them down into their components or aspects. It's part of our culture to do this. Read this paragraph once more; it is at the heart of my message.

Take computers, for example. If someone who knew nothing about them asked you about computers, no doubt you would follow your instincts and immediately begin by dividing them into their constituent pieces or aspects: hardware, software, and telecommunications, perhaps. Or maybe your instinct is to separate the computer into monitor, keyboard, hard drive,

floppy drive, mouse, printer, cables, software, memory, and chips. Or perhaps you might think of the computer as composed of plastic, silicon, metals, rubber, and glass. It depends on your aptitude or inclination. These are all, however, examples of *thinking downward* first.

My belief is that it is vital to think in context first. The dictionary defines the word "context" as "all of the circumstances and conditions surrounding and influencing an event or object." Thinking in context does not preclude thinking downward. It just delays this step and adds a first step of thinking upward by asking a *critical question*.

What Is the Item Itself a Part Of?

If you think about computers in context, the question is "What is the computer a part of?" The answer could be "Information Processing." But you may have a different answer, and there is nothing wrong with that, just as long as you have thought in context first. By first asking what the item under discussion is a part of—no matter whether it is a computer, a car steering wheel, a person, or a film—you can begin to build a hierarchy or an inverted tree-structure.

It's very similar to building a family tree, and that's a good exercise to start with. Who and what are *you?* What are *you* a part of? Take a piece of blank paper, write your name in the very middle of it, and draw a box around it. Now draw a vertical line upward from that box and draw another box with the words "Human Being" in it. Continue to "think up" and diagram the results.

Look at Diagram A on page 12. Can you see that looking at yourself in context **first** enables you to begin seeing relationships that were not apparent before? Does it also begin to prompt ideas when you look at yourself in context? Does it spark your imagination?

This is part of the method I call *"Thinking Around the Box™."* Others to whom I have taught this method for analysis have called it *"360-Degree Thinking."* One of my students called it her *"Secret Weapon."* In any event it is *not* thinking inside the box.

You would not start building a family tree by putting your name at the top of a piece of paper, would you? If you do not have children yet, then your name would be the only one appearing on the paper. What matters in a family tree are those who came before. It's the same with everything. Where a subject comes from, or what it is a part of—in other words, its context—influences where it is going.

Diagram A

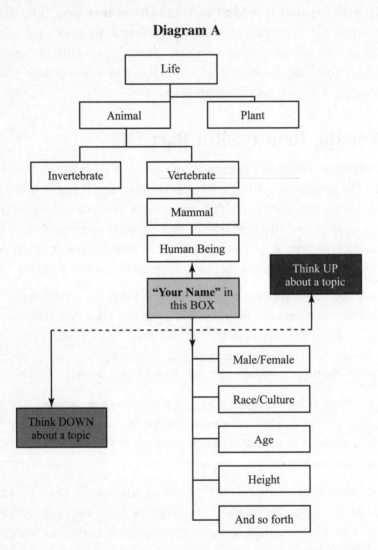

You can now see—by means of this simple graphic—the opportunities afforded to you by thinking in context. You can also draw horizontal lines that divide the animal kingdom or mammals into categories, or you can keep on going up and discover what animals are a part of. Before long, you have created your own personal classification. (Warning, do not go on *ad infinitum*.) Once you are finished thinking up, it makes sense to break down the bottom category—*you*.

Next, try putting the word "Computer" in the middle of a page and drawing a line upward and writing the words "Information Processing" above it. See how far you can go up *before* breaking the computer down into its parts.

Get a group of friends or family members together, choose the main word or words from one of the sample essay topics in Chapter 12, and brainstorm with the group to come up with what the word is a part of. For beginners, contextual thinking is not an easy process; practicing in a group with a dictionary, a thesaurus, and an encyclopedia will help. You will find three examples of brainstorming the key words in an essay question in Chapter 11.

Now, take a piece of paper and try this exercise again, this time by thinking about a steering wheel in its context. Usually when we hear or see the words "steering wheel," our imagination sees only an assortment of plastic, aluminum, nuts, bolts, leather, chrome, buttons, icons, and so on. However, if you think about the same item in context first, you will soon be seeing it as first and foremost an integral part of a car. You can then easily see that a car is a part of our transportation system. Remember to start at the bottom and work up.

You can see the diagram I came up with on the following page.

Diagram B

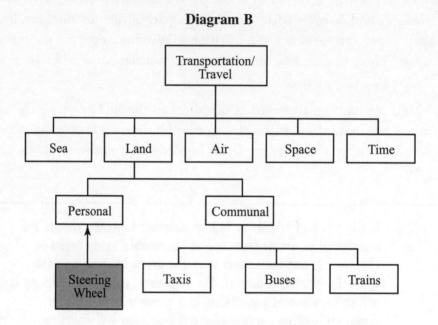

I hope that you can now see the relevance of looking at things this way. I said at the beginning that the first, vital step in the process of writing is **discovery through exploration.** Thinking in context helps you discover much more about the item in question.

Not looking at something in context is the equivalent of viewing a 6-foot by 6-foot painting only from a vantage point 6 inches away from the canvas. How much can you know or discover about a painting that is 36 square feet in area if you stand so close? Wouldn't you initially and instinctively stand some distance back and take in the painting in all its glory before moving closer to look at a detail? It is the same for a steering wheel, computer, geranium, or almost anything else, including the most important subject—you. Looking at yourself from a distance means being objective, and that is crucial to understanding yourself.

In the body of this book, I hope to show you that thinking in context has many advantages—and not just when you are writing an essay. Thinking in context gives you a framework that you can use to help you systematize the process of thinking about writing. It will help you to develop a point of view, and it certainly provokes and stimulates creative and critical thinking by forcing your imagination into top gear.

So, since the subject of this book is the essay, let's now think about essays themselves by using the contextual thinking part of *Thinking Around the Box*™. Write the word "Essay" in the middle of a page and draw a box around it. Look up the word "essay" in the dictionary and you will find that essays are a form of writing. This sounds obvious, but we often overlook the obvious, and that's the point of contextual thinking: meaning becomes a lot clearer when something is viewed in context. Now, draw a vertical line above the word "Essay" in its box and write the word "Writing" in another box.

Diagram C

Look up the word "writing" in an encyclopedia, and you will discover that there are two types of writing: public and private. This means that you now have to insert another level between the word "Essay" and the word "Writing." You can understand now why it's a good idea to always use pencil when doing this.

Diagram D

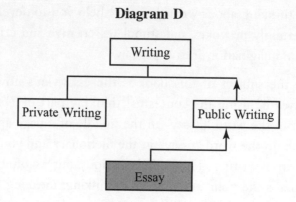

Now you have the word "Writing" with two vertical lines beneath it. One says "Private Writing," the other says "Public Writing." The word "Essay" should now appear beneath "Public Writing," since essays—unlike diaries, journals, and practice writing—are meant to be seen by others, as are novels, plays, journalism, poetry, and history books. These last-named categories can now be placed beneath "Public Writing," on the same level as essays.

Diagram E

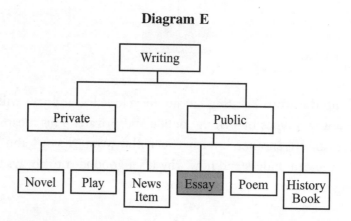

Now, going back up the hierarchy that you are building, ask the question "What is writing itself a part of?" "Communications" is my answer, and let's say that is the top of the pyramid for now. If I now analyze the term "communications," I can quickly deduce that it has at least five parts and only one of them is writing:

1. We can communicate an idea by *numbers*. For example, "The price of the laptop is $799.00."

2. We can communicate by *writing*.

3. We can communicate by *speaking,* either *verbally* or by *sign language.*

4. We regularly communicate by using either *moving* or *static images,* which can be worth a thousand words.

5. We can also communicate by *musical notation,* which can then be performed by a voice or manufactured instruments to communicate some of the most powerful messages and emotions known to us.

Once I had thought about essays and concluded that they were a part of public writing and that writing was a kind of communication, I opened two books, a dictionary and an encyclopedia. Always have a dictionary and an encyclopedia handy, if allowed.

This is what I found out: *"Communication: The act of transmission, sharing, or the exchange of ideas, thoughts, messages, and information by signals, speech, and writing."* This, of course, prompted a thought that communications include such ancient methods as smoke signals, flags, gestures, and even facial expressions that had to suffice before the Internet was invented. So here it is, Diagram F, a fully-thought-out example of contextual thinking. Study it.

Diagram F

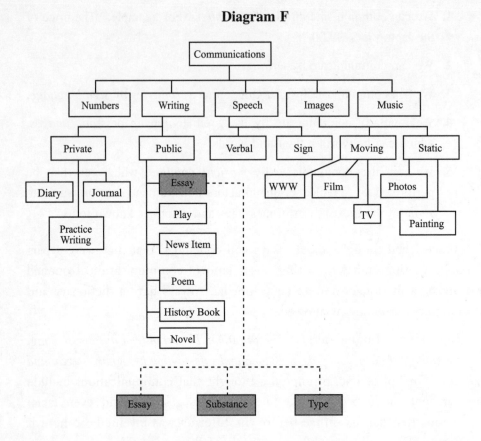

Earlier, I quite deliberately violated my own first principle; I broke down the idea of the essay into three parts—style, substance, and type—without first thinking about the idea of an essay in its context. Now that we have the essay set into its proper context, it is finally time to break down the word "Essay" into its constituent parts of style, substance, and type, as shown in Diagram F above.

Some of you who have studied biology or botany might recognize this kind of classification as taxonomy. The topmost item on the hierarchy or pyramid is the most inclusive or least specific, such as "Communications" in the previous example. Just saying that something living is, for example, an animal, does not say much, except that it is not a plant. The lowest item or division is the least inclusive or most specific. All thoughts, ideas, and facts are made up of component parts and are also part of something bigger. **Always examine both aspects.**

Contextual thinking is simply an effort to organize your thoughts about *anything*—a computer, yourself, the essay, the town you live in, a geranium, or a Jeep—this same way. This kind of thinking has been useful to all kinds of successful people—warriors, diplomats, politicians, and business-people—and the lack of this kind of thinking has hindered many unsuccessful people and perhaps even been the cause of their failure. The worlds of diplomacy, politics, and war-making are full of examples of shortsightedness, usually caused by breaking down information before looking at it in its larger context first.

A good example is the movie business, which we think of as being one of the most successful businesses ever. However, most of those involved always thought of themselves as being *only* in the movie-making business. If they had thought in context, they would have realized that they were in the entertainment business instead, and by now they might have owned pieces of the TV, radio, music, magazine, and theater businesses too. Try diagramming this example as an exercise in contextual thinking. It's a case study at Harvard Business School.

Some call contextual thinking strategic. I call it common sense. Why? Because nothing exists in a vacuum or in isolation. Connections make the world make sense, so it makes sense to first discover and then examine them. After all, an ostrich with its head buried in the sand is hardly in a position to look at the big picture.

Freewriting

As you are drawing the boxes on paper, be aware of ideas as they come to you. They *will* come because the act of thinking in context provokes them. Be more than just aware of them, focus on them. This is your imagination at work. Having encouraged you to follow the process of thinking about things in context first, now comes the best piece of advice I can offer.

When you are first presented with an idea about which you must write an essay, some very valuable information will begin to spring to mind. This will happen continuously as you look at the words in the essay question and as you think about the subject in context. The information will take the form of random ideas, imaginings, musings, feelings, stirrings, and conjectures—call them what you will. These unformed thoughts will come instinctively. Trust them. Blurt them out and write them down on separate notes. If you are in the SAT/ACT Assessment exam room, you will need to use the paper at hand for these notes. However, if you are writing a college application essay, write your notes on separate pieces of paper or self-stick removable notes. **Capture these thoughts at all costs.** This part of the process is called "freewriting." When freewriting, don't worry about grammar, spelling, or thinking up or down or even sideways. This is a case of speak before you think. Just capture the thoughts as they come. Capture them, for as a wise man once said, "Thoughts fly, but words go on foot." As I write, a book is at the top of the *New York Times* best seller list in the nonfiction category. Its title is *Blink* and its author, Malcolm Gladwell, comes very close to proving that our instinct, or hunches, or sixth sense, is frequently right.

Later, we will discuss in more detail the fact that the essay is, at its heart, the expression of a point of view: *your* point of view. Looking at a subject from all angles will help you develop a comprehensive perspective on the topic and make your point of view more easily developed. Thinking in context with diagramming and freewriting will help to nurture the originality and creativity with which you write.

As an exercise, try putting the word "Gardens" in context and practice freewriting as ideas come along. On the next page, draw and fill in boxes above "Gardens" as you answer the question "What are gardens a part of?"

Gardens

If you think in context about gardens, you will begin to think in terms of food as well as flowers, seeds, fertilizer, and mowers. You may have memories of childhood or survival of a disaster. It also pays to look through the eyes of others when examining a topic. Your parents may find beauty and comfort in their garden, while an environmentalist may view it as toxic or wasteful. Gardens have had unintended consequences: the shortage of water has become critical in Nevada and Arizona because people have been growing lawns without considering the impact that may have on their environment.

Are you now convinced that you can think more creatively and with more originality by taking this step of thinking upward first instead of downward? If so, let's build on that skill by examining the next new way of thinking.

CRITICAL THINKING

First of all, let me clear up a misunderstanding. Critical thinking does not mean learning to find fault. We all already know, all too well, how to do that. Critical thinking means learning to think a little differently by reading between the lines. It means searching for truth and meaning by being open to discovery: a closed mind never moved humanity forward by an inch. Quite the opposite is true.

Critical thinking is a skill that can be learned and should be learned. Critical thinking begins by thinking about thinking, and this is not a simple matter. It is, however, a vital one. You need to concentrate now. If everything in the world had an obvious meaning that everyone agreed upon, then there would be no room for interpretation, would there? For example, if everyone in the world were in agreement on the role of government, then there would be no need of political parties. If we all agreed on what was good art and bad art or what constituted good music or high fashion or the perfect car, then life would be very different from what we now experience every day. In a word, our world would be boring, and it isn't, or at least it shouldn't be.

One reality you already know is that the world is a vast and complex place. Because of this fact, it is tempting to let others do the thinking about it. Don't! Another reality is that we all have more potential ability to think about our world and our place in it than we realize. We only need to unlock that potential. This is where critical thinking comes in. Follow along as we explore the notion.

First, let's look at some basics to help you understand the magic that is critical thinking. When researchers and philosophers discover new ideas, concepts, or rules, the fact that they are new, and of course have never been given names before, means that the discoverer or inventor gets to do the honors. After all, an idea without a name would be too difficult and time-consuming to transmit easily. The inventors of cars would have had a hard time explaining, let alone selling, their invention if they constantly had to refer to it as a "self-propelled, four-wheeled, horseless carriage that utilizes a petroleum-fueled, internal combustion engine, a gearbox, and a transmission." Thank goodness someone thought up the words "automobile" and "car."

Similarly, we have to deal with the first psychologists who called the mental process that controls our ability to think "cognition." They did so in the interests of brevity and clarity; they simply had to come up with a single word that substituted for nine: "The mental process that controls our ability to think."

Examining this mental process further, these psychologists found out that we are rather like computers. We get our information about the world through our five senses: sight, smell, touch, hearing, and taste. Our cognitive abilities (our computers) allow us to process that information, which resides in our brain as images. Without this faculty, we would neither be able to make decisions nor tell others of them. So it's quite important to understand this much about cognition, wouldn't you agree?

So what is thinking, then? Thinking happens when we simply manipulate images of information within our brain. These images represent abstract information, and thinking about the relationships between these images helps us make decisions, solve problems, reach conclusions, answer questions, and reach our goals. Somehow, in a mysterious process that is not fully understood, we tend to group images that seem to belong together into what psychologists call "concepts." These are the building blocks of rational thinking, and as a human you are uniquely gifted with the skill of creating and using them.

Rational or logical thinking, sometimes called *reasoning,* leads to conclusions that are well-thought-out. If you write an essay that does not come to a rational conclusion, you will have failed the first test. Colleges and employers prize reasoning skills because they lead to good decision-making, and good decision-making earns their trust.

Types of Reasoning

There are two types of reasoning. The first, *deductive reasoning,* is an ancient idea. It was first brought to our attention more than 2,300 years ago in Aristotle's famous piece of deductive reasoning, which he called a syllogism. We also call it syllogistic logic. This is what he said, and it changed the world's way of thinking: "All men are mortal; Aristotle is a man; therefore, Aristotle is mortal." In other words, if all men die, and I am a man, then so will I. By the way, Aristotle proved this point by passing on in 322 B.C.

To this day, this same logic is used in all kinds of fields, such as engineering, the law, military strategy, and diplomacy. Deductive reasoning involves assumptions, or premises, and applies a generalization to a specific instance. A specific premise is true (I am a human), a general premise is also true (all humans die), so a conclusion that is also true can be drawn, applying the general to the specific (I will die). This is powerful stuff!

The second type of reasoning, *inductive reasoning,* makes a generalization based on a large number of individual observations. These observations crystallize into generalization so rapidly that the process may be described as your intuition at work. Although inductive reasoning is a sort of mirror image of deductive reasoning, its intuitive nature makes it almost instantaneous. Intuition happens so quickly, in fact, that you are unaware that you are stepping through the process of thinking. **Intuition is reason in a hurry.** My advice is to trust your intuition. Hunches are frequent visitors in our lives, and no one can prove that they are any less valid than reasoned thinking.

The result of all this thinking about what we know and what we don't know is first problem-solving and then decision-making. What we are doing, whether we know it or not, is following rules. Instinctively, we go through the following steps:

1. We prepare by analyzing the situation.

2. We list alternative solutions.

3. We evaluate all possible solutions.

4. We select one and then we act.

Then we do it all again.

If you think about it, soccer or hockey players go through this sequence of steps hundreds of times in a game. They have to make quick decisions about where and how to move next, and players have only seconds or less to go through all four steps.

Writing an essay is more deliberate than playing soccer. If you are not careful to take the steps noted above before actually writing, the person marking your essay will know immediately. If you begin to write without analyzing (thinking in context) first, listing the options, and evaluating them before choosing one and acting on it, you will lose out to the 5 or 10 essay writers who do follow the recommended steps and win the million dollar prize.

 Once you see the topic about which you are to write, take a deep breath and slow down. Read the topic several times—out loud if you can. This will help you understand what the topic is about and, just as importantly, what it is *not* about. You would be staggered to learn how many students answer the wrong topic; the one they misread or thought they read. No matter how good the essay, if you answer the wrong topic, you have left the examiner with little option but to fail you. If you scan the topic quickly, breathe a sigh of relief that it is something that you know a little about, and immediately start writing, you risk the same result.

Prewriting

Prewriting is a vital component of critical thinking and **always comes first**—before you begin writing the essay itself. In an SAT/ACT Assessment timed essay, you will have very little time for prewriting, but be sure to do it anyway. Notice that the steps that follow are very similar to the process we discussed under contextual thinking. We are simply developing them further, in critical thinking terms.

First, begin by analyzing the situation. This encompasses thinking in context first—upward, then downward—and freewriting your thoughts, intuitions, and hunches as you do.

Second, ask yourself what you still don't know about the topic and freewrite your answers.

Third, group all these ideas into categories. This is vital since these groupings can become the basis for your paragraphs. If you are not writing a timed essay, using separate pieces of paper or self-stick removable notes can be very helpful.

People who are good critical thinkers employ some tricks. For example, if you have written a note that says "Dogs are man's best friends," turn it into a question: "Are dogs man's best friends?" That way, you will raise some issues you can explore and freewrite as you do. Perhaps you might conclude that cattle, cats, or camels, not dogs, have had that honor over the years. That kind of musing would be considered both original and creative!

The more time you spend planning, the easier the actual composition will be. Finally, act upon your thoughts and write your essay—more on this later.

Critical Thinking Tips

❑ **Try to think without conventional constraints.** For example, if a burglar invaded your home, you would not hesitate to use a brick as a weapon. You would not stop to consider whether the brick's sole purpose is to help build a house and is therefore off-limits as a means of self-defense. You would pick it up and use it as a weapon. Watch a child use anything—a cardboard box, for instance—to climb up to the cookie jar without considering the original intended purpose of the box. We lose that instinct as we grow, except when a burglar is in the house, of course!

❑ **Being emotional is the opposite of thinking critically.** The only time for "being emotional" in an essay is when you declare the foregoing fact in your opening sentence.

❑ **If the logic of your argument comes apart at any stage, start over.** Nothing is worse than tortured logic that attempts to prove a point with flawed evidence or reasoning; you will recognize it, and the examiner will also. Preparation will minimize the chances of this happening.

❑ **If you state something as being true, make sure it is.** There are relatively few universal truths, such as 8 plus 2 equals 10. A fact is as true in Tokyo as it is in Timbuktu, Toledo, or Tampa.

❑ **Note that the opposite of universal truth is not fiction, but taste.** Personal preference, or taste, is rarely if ever agreed upon. Taste is far from true or universal, and that is something that is crucial for you to understand. The color lavender or a particular kind of music may seem uplifting or enjoyable to one person, but not to another. Assuming that your reader's taste is identical to yours is a sure route to failure. By the way, just because you like lavender does not mean that someone who dislikes it is wrong—they just have different taste.

❑ **Be careful, even skeptical, about sources of information.** This approach is another important ingredient to critical thinking. If you want the truth about why your friend dumped you, don't ask your friend. He or she will want to make you feel better, not to tell you the truth: "He's a jerk, you're a treasure." Did you learn something from that advice, or did you just feel better, and which is more important?

CREATIVE THINKING

Creative thinking is the twin sister of critical thinking, or perhaps the other side of the same coin. Not a great deal is known about the human creative spark. Nevertheless, I will claim from experience that if you pay attention to the first two of these new ways of *Thinking Around the Box*™—contextual and critical—and if you practice them diligently, then you will have prepared yourself to be more creative. In other words, getting into the habit of looking at ideas, things, and people in context and becoming open to new ways of thinking about things will, with the help of hard work and practice, spark your imagination. After all, it is imagination, coupled with working diligently and persistently, that wins Nobel prizes and changes the course of history.

For tens of thousands of years, our ancestors thought of rivers only as places to fish and slake their thirst. Then, a long time after another person invented the wheel, someone imagined that perhaps the river's power could be used in place of man power or woman power to turn a wheel. Soon after, the wheel of a water mill was milling flour.

Someone else wondered why people were constantly following migratory herds of animals. He or she had the courage to imagine what it would be like if crops were sown and harvested, if animals were tamed, herded together, and hence always available to provide hides and wool for clothing and shelter, meat and milk for food, and their strength for laborious tasks. They started the process of settled living, and humans ever after have been free to pursue other activities. Now that is what I call creative thinking!

These and other sparks of imagination changed the course of history. Try thinking of other leaps of imagination—harnessing electricity, inventing the internal combustion engine, creating nuclear power—and write an essay about how they changed the course of history, putting the event in context first, of course.

A simple first step toward thinking creatively is accepting that you can do it. Remember that you are in possession of the most complex entity in the universe—your brain. It still remains a dream of computer scientists to build a machine that comes close to mimicking even a few of the brain's abilities. Your brain is capable of amazing feats. It makes you self-aware. It allows you to speak and learn and make sense of the world. It thinks in color. It assembles seemingly unrelated facts and permits you to draw conclusions from them. It can look at options to help you choose. It can look at the future and model it for you by asking and answering "what if" questions. It is also your seat of inspiration. And it's all yours to use, train, and use some more—or not. You alone can choose the option to think. Your parents, teachers, or even bosses can't force this responsibility on you.

Your Creativity

Most geniuses are quite modest. The immodest ones tend not to be geniuses at all, just self-promoters. Anyway, geniuses tend to suggest that 90 percent of inspiration comes from just showing up to work, and work and still more work brings inspiration. The most famous was Edison, who said "Genius is 1 percent inspiration and 99 percent perspiration." Being lazy, it seems, is no way to seek inspiration, and idling never feeds imagination.

As I said before, intuition is reason in a hurry. If you feel or hear an idea coming, write it down at once. Don't ever let it go. "Write before you think" could be your motto. It is crucial to write these thoughts down as they are blurted out from somewhere deep in your subconscious. You can evaluate them later and choose the best rough diamonds to polish. We all instinctively process information as soon as we gather it. A foul smell from a milk carton intuitively warns us that illness would follow consumption of the spoiled milk. This process does not even rise to the level of thought. It's our immune system giving us an early warning, and we trust it implicitly. Why not trust our sixth sense when it comes to the realm of ideas?

The next time someone says something interesting or controversial, listen to your immediate, involuntary response and note it. Don't just remain vaguely aware; that inkling somewhere in the back of your mind is the voice of your imagination. Listen to it. In fact, do all you can to let it get louder; remove all obstacles to its surfacing. Treasure it. It's your instinct, your creative voice calling.

By the way, don't throw away the ideas that seem to contradict your belief. They could become useful later as ways to prove your point. A good tactic in both debates and essay writing is to state an objection to your position and then demolish it.

The question, therefore, is not whether you are creative and capable of original thinking. If you are a human being, you are. The better question is this: "What can I do to provoke and harness my imagination?" The answer lies in thinking differently; in context, critically, and creatively—*Thinking Around the Box*™. Think around all of the compass points—all 360 of them.

One important piece of advice: the more you know, the more you *will* know and the more likely you will be to create. Acquiring knowledge is like adding fuel to the fire of your imagination, and writing gives that learning a purpose. Read, listen, debate, discuss, and remain open to new ideas and you *will* write well, as long as you also learn to follow the rules that are described in later chapters and practice, practice, practice.

In Short

1. An essay has three aspects: **Style, Substance,** and **Type.**

2. Style is *how* you write. Substance is *what* you write about. Essays can be of two types: *informative* or *persuasive.* (See Chapter 5)

3. *Thinking Around the Box*™ requires looking at topics in context first.

4. As you do this, ideas will flow. Write them down. They are like gold. Intuition is reason in a hurry.

5. *Thinking Around the Box*™—contextual thinking, critical thinking, and creative thinking—will help you be more imaginative and original.

CHAPTER THREE

Basics of Essay Composition

Now you know that *Thinking Around the Box*™ is crucial to the discovery phase of essay writing as I approach it. What about the disclosure phase? What is an essay, anyway? What should it look like and what does it contain?

WHAT IS AN ESSAY?

I can think of no better example of a great essay than the Prologue to Bertrand Russell's autobiography. Russell was a complex person—a political and social activist, a mathematical and philosophical genius, and a dedicated humanitarian. He won the Nobel Prize for literature in 1950 and died in 1970. This is what he wrote:

essay

What I Have Lived For

Three passions, simple but overwhelmingly strong have governed my life: the longing for love, the search for knowledge, and unbearable pity for the suffering of mankind. These passions, like great winds, have blown me hither and thither, in a wayward course, over a deep ocean of anguish, reaching to the very verge of despair.

I have sought love, first, because it brings ecstasy—ecstasy so great that I would often have sacrificed the rest of life for a few hours of this joy. I have sought it, next, because it relieves loneliness—that terrible loneliness in which one shivering consciousness looks over the rim of the world into the cold unfathomable lifeless abyss. I have sought it, finally, because in the union of love I have seen, in a mystic miniature, the prefiguring vision of the heaven that saints and poets have imagined. This is what I sought, and though it might seem too good for human life, this is what—at last—I have found.

With equal passion I have sought knowledge. I have wished to understand the hearts of men. I have wished to know why the stars shine. And I have tried to apprehend the Pythagorean power by which number holds sway above the flux. A little of this, but not much, I have achieved.

Love and knowledge, so far as they were possible, led upward toward the heavens. But always pity brought me back to Earth. Echoes of cries of pain reverberate in my heart. Children in famine, victims tortured by oppressors, helpless old people a hated burden to their sons, and the whole world of loneliness, poverty, and pain make a mockery of what human life should be. I long to alleviate the evil, but I cannot, and I too suffer.

This has been my life. I have found it worth living and would gladly live it again if the chance were offered me.

I am sure that you have noticed that the language of this essay is a little antique and flowery, as well as passionate. Nevertheless, I am also sure that having finished reading Russell's essay, you now know the man. He told you who he was by explaining his beliefs about his reasons for living. This is very like what you must do: tell your readers something about yourself by stating a viewpoint and developing it. Believe in yourself—you are worth it.

An essay may be characterized as short, nonfiction prose that conveys a personal point of view. By the way, the English word "essay" comes from the French word "essai," which means "to try or attempt."

For the purposes of this book, we will assume that short means 5 to 10 paragraphs and 250 to 500 words. The word count really depends on whether the essay is written for the SAT or ACT Assessment, where you have 25 or 30 minutes, respectively, or a college entrance application, where you have unlimited time.

Nonfiction means what it says. The essay should not be a fictional story. This does not mean that you must never write a short piece of fiction—just don't call it an essay or submit it in response to an essay prompt.

Prose is the language of everyday conventional speech (definitely without using the "likes" and "you knows" of today's vernacular, however). Prose should never be flowery or ornate. It usually contains very few figures of speech, such as metaphors. It avoids unnecessary adverbs (words that describe verbs) and adjectives (words that describe nouns). There will be more on this later. What matters is not the number of words, but how easily the essay takes readers from start to finish while making sure they understand everything in between.

A personal point of view is simply an opinion, or thesis. Previous chapters were all about thinking your way to an opinion.

The first sentence of your first paragraph in each essay you write is the statement of the point of view. It is called the **thesis** statement. The secret to good essay writing is to have something to say and to say it as clearly as you can. Having something to say means developing an idea about a point of view. Saying it clearly means obeying the laws of style when expressing that idea.

What really matters to the reader is the message, otherwise known as your point of view, or thesis. Style—how you write—will enhance the delivery of your message, if it is well executed; however, it will get in the way of communicating your message if it is poorly executed. **The most important objectives in essay composition are finding (discovering) something to say and sharing it with (or disclosing it to) your reader.**

Look at style this way: What happens if the singer of your favorite band begins to sing off key? You cringe and your attention is immediately diverted away from the song's message and toward the mistake. An experienced reader of English will have a similarly jarring experience if what he or she is reading is incorrectly expressed. "We was the happiest pair, just like them lovebirds we sees come Spring." A lovely sentiment, no doubt, but the reader will not hear the message because it breaks so many rules of good writing style.

Clarity, not ambiguity, is your goal. Consider the following sentence from a long-ago tourism brochure. "The population of London is very dense." Did the writer intend to inform the reader that there are a lot of Londoners living in a small space? Or was the writer of the brochure perhaps excusing the behavior of Londoners, in advance, by telling his readers that they are rather unintelligent?

The purpose of writing is to reveal something of yourself to the reader. You do not want that to include a lack of understanding of the basic rules of grammar, syntax, and punctuation.

WHAT SHOULD AN ESSAY LOOK LIKE?

If you have ever been on a debate team, you probably know the three rules of debating:

1. Tell them what you are going to say.

2. Say it.

3. Tell them what you have said.

This assumes, of course, that the debater has come to a definite opinion on the topic. The principle is the same for an essay. Let's say you have been asked to write about the fact that honesty is the best policy. After you have thought about the issue in context in a disciplined way and come to a point of view, you tell your readers what you are about to say and suggest the proofs you are going to use. You do this in your thesis sentence.

You then use the sentences in each of your next few paragraphs to support and demonstrate, and perhaps prove the validity of, your position. In the last paragraph, you summarize the argument. We will get back to that in more detail later.

So this is how you should proceed:

1. Think about what you are going to say.

2. Tell your readers what you believe.

3. Support and demonstrate it.

4. Prove it valid (perhaps).

5. Then summarize it.

THE STRUCTURE OF THE ESSAY

You probably know all this anyway, but the following needs to be stated so that you will have a reference. Several sentences make a paragraph and several paragraphs make an essay. A good pattern or structure for an essay is 1-3-1, in other words, one paragraph that introduces the reader to your point of view (thesis) and spells out the beginning of your support for your thesis, followed by three body/support paragraphs and one concluding paragraph. There is some debate over whether this format is the best one; some excellent essays may have more support paragraphs, but not many have fewer. I believe that you will have the best chance of success, especially in a timed examination, with the 1-3-1 essay, so I advise you to master this pattern first. Your teacher or parents may differ on this point. In any case, if you have not gone through the process of developing a personal opinion or point of view, the essay format will not matter, since your voice will seem inauthentic.

A sentence is a string of words that expresses a complete thought or idea. A sentence must contain a **subject,** that is, a noun or pronoun that specifies the person, thing, or place that is the subject of the sentence. To find the subject of a sentence, ask yourself who or what the sentence is about. In the sentence "Mary works two jobs," the subject is "Mary," a noun. In the sentence "I work two jobs," the subject is the pronoun, "I." By the way, the other personal pronouns are: *me, you, she, her, he, him, it, we, us, they,* and *them.*

A sentence must also contain a verb. There are three kinds of verbs. An **action verb** tells the reader what the subject does; in the sentence above about Mary, the action verb is "works."

The second kind of verb is called a **linking verb.** No action is performed by this verb. In the sentence "The game is lost," the word "is" simply links the subject ("the game") to a word that describes it. Some other linking verbs are: *am, are, was, were, seem, seems, seemed, become, becomes,* and *became.* Still linking verbs that describe senses are: *look, looks, looked, appear, appears, appeared, smell, smells, smelled, taste, tastes, tasted, sound, sounds, sounded, feel, feels,* and *felt.*

The third kind of verb is the **helping verb.** Consider the difference between "I learn" and "I am learning." The verb "am" helps the other verb "learning." Some other helping verbs are: are, been, being, is, was, were, have, has, had, do, does, did, can, could, may, might, must, should, will, and would. These verbs can be used alone but are usually used with other verbs to change voice, tense, or mood.

If you write a string of words and then a period or a question mark indicating the end of a sentence, make sure that the idea is a complete one. For example, "I get the feeling" is not a complete idea. "I get the feeling that you are unhappy" is a complete sentence.

A paragraph is a group of sentences that work together to make a point. The first sentence of the paragraph is the **topic sentence.** It states the main point you are going to make in the paragraph. If it is the first sentence of the opening paragraph of an essay, it is also called the **thesis sentence** because it states your proposition, sometimes called the **controlling idea.** It tells your audience what position you are going to take and, quite possibly, prove to be valid.

The ideal thesis statement not only makes your proposition (point of view, thesis, or controlling idea) clear, but it should also contain the seeds of the ideas that you are going to go on to explain or use to prove your point. It is your theme and a preview of things to come. "I believe that school uniforms benefit both the students and the school by improving discipline, reducing or eliminating social distinctions, and improving the learning environment." In this opening thesis sentence, the reader is left in no doubt about the writer's position (school uniforms are a good idea) and the topics of the next three paragraphs are introduced (discipline, social distinctions, and the learning environment). The writer has alerted the reader to the fact that the topics of the paragraphs will be discipline, social distinctions, and the learning environment. Now, the reader can expect these points to be supported and demonstrated, possibly even proved, and a final paragraph will tie it all together.

The next sentences in a paragraph are called **body** or **support sentences.** There are usually three to five of them and they contain facts, quotations, statistics, and other details to support the topic sentence. The final sentence in the paragraph is the **concluding sentence.** This reminds the reader of the main point of the paragraph by making a point.

The sentence is like a mini-paragraph. The paragraph is like a mini-essay. Just as the topic sentence states the case for the paragraph, the first paragraph with its thesis statement states the case for the essay. The second, third, and fourth paragraphs are support or body paragraphs. They include their own topic sentences, support sentences, and concluding sentences.

In Short

1. Essays reflect your interior self, just as surely as a mirror reflects your exterior self.

2. Essays are nonfiction, written in everyday language, and express and support your point of view.

3. Style supports substance. A clear style will help communicate the most important factor: your message.

4. Develop your thesis or point of view first. Make sure it contains not only your thesis, but the seeds of the ideas that you will develop. Now state it, support and demonstrate it, and prove it. Finally, summarize it.

5. The sentence is like a small paragraph. The paragraph is like a small essay.

CHAPTER FOUR

Theory into Practice

Let's say that you are asked to write a 1-3-1 essay on the following topic: *The invention of television has been of benefit to society. Agree or disagree.* How should you proceed?

FOLLOW THE STEPS

1. Contextual Thinking. Make sure you employ the contextual thinking technique, thinking upward first. Write the initials "TV" in the middle of a piece of paper and ask yourself what television is a part of. I did this and came up with the following answer: I think it is part of our modern information delivery systems. So I wrote the words "Information Delivery Systems" above "TV."

Diagram G

In thinking some more about the topic, I realized that there are two basic types of information delivery systems. There are those that are broadcast one-way, such as newspapers, books, radio, and, of course, television. There are also information systems that are two-way or bi-directional. You might call them interactive. The World Wide Web and the telephone are the best examples.

So now, on my piece of paper, I have "Information Delivery Systems" at the top, with two vertical lines beneath it. At the foot of one line it says "Two-Way Systems," and at the foot of the other it says "One-Way Systems." Each of these headings is, in turn, subdivided with more vertical lines descending from them. "WWW" and the "Phone" are under "Two-Way Systems," and "Newspapers," "Books," "Radios," and "TV" are under "One-Way Systems."

Diagram H

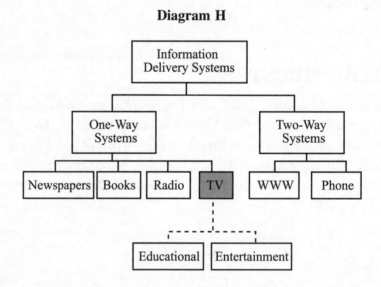

It took only a couple of minutes to think of television in its context and sketch it out on a note pad. Not much effort, really.

2. Constituent Parts. Now, you can go ahead and begin breaking down television into its constituent parts. Since you are thinking in context, you will not be tempted to break down television into its physical components. At this point, you are looking at it as a distribution vehicle, not just a box. So, in the context of an information distribution appliance, what capabilities does it have? My answer is that television can broadcast two types of information: educational and entertainment. I have added that underneath "TV" in Diagram H above. Now you have TV in its context.

3. Turn the Topic into a Question. Having examined television in context, turn the essay topic into a question. Has the invention of television been of benefit to society? Do not answer with a yes or a no. Instead, listen to your intuition. Asking this question will—or at least should—prompt some ideas, thoughts, and conjectures on the subject. Be sure to write these down. I emphasize that this is the time to freewrite. This is not the time to decide on a position one way or the other.

As you freewrite ideas, place a notation alongside your thought that indicates whether the idea supports the notion of television being beneficial or not: perhaps a 'Y' for yes, an 'N' for no, and '?' if you don't know yet.

I did this. It took less than 5 minutes and here is what I came up with:

➤ Commercials ruin the experience. N

➤ TV is used too little for education, yet it is an ideal medium for it. N

➤ Personal video recorders will help TV fulfill its potential. Y

➤ TV relaxes people. Y

➤ TV is good company for those who live alone. Y

➤ TV frequently promotes anti-social behavior. N

➤ The overall quality of the programming is poor. N

➤ TV makes people lazy. N

➤ TV watching is a passive activity. It discourages exercise and encourages eating the bad foods advertised. N

➤ TV has discouraged reading, conversation, and eating together as a family. N

These ten ideas, thoughts, and conjectures came to mind in a matter of minutes. Seven are negative votes, three are positive votes. Does this mean that I should take the thesis position in my essay that television has not been a benefit to society? Not necessarily. Remember that you can use statements such as TV promotes bad behavior and argue against it to make your point.

Now, focus on the ideas you have written down by putting them into groups and seeing which group—the pros or the cons—gets your vote. At the very least, you now have some support sentences all ready as well as support paragraphs. The skeleton of your essay just wrote itself! Well, almost.

I took my ten notes (I use self-stick removable notes, but any separate pieces of paper will do) and sorted them into groups and read them over again. All that was left for me to do was to string these ideas together into an essay composed of topic sentences, support sentences, and conclusions.

4. Write. Here's an example of a finished essay about television, incorporating the ideas that resulted from thinking in context, with a point of view that resulted from the process.

essay

The invention of television has been of benefit to society. Agree or disagree.

The invention of television has had a largely negative impact on society. (*Thesis Sentence*) Although television is a medium that is ideally suited for educational purposes, it has largely failed to fulfill that mission. Television watching replaces healthy social interactions in the home, discourages healthy physical activity, and promotes poor eating habits. (*2 Support Sentences*)

Television is a perfect medium for education, but few television networks devote much time to educational programming. (*Topic Sentence*) For every nature program or cultural event, there are hundreds of shows that are anything but educational. These shows often test the boundaries of what is acceptable in terms of sex and violence. In fact, bad taste in television commercials and programming seems to be the rule rather than the exception, especially during "prime time." (*3 Support Sentences*)

Television has also eroded the time available to devote to social exchange at home. (*Topic Sentence*) Taking up more and more of people's time, it has discouraged individuals from reading. Because scheduling frequently involves viewing plans, it has too often discouraged families from eating together. With commercials and program-ming more likely to stun rather than stimulate, television has also discouraged the exchange of ideas in conversation. (*3 Support Sentences*)

No less important, television promotes some very unhealthy behavior. (*Topic Sentence*) It does not involve the viewer because it cannot; it is a one-way system. It needs the audience to be passive and uninvolved, but receptive. The companies that own this service view it as a marketing tool, so that is what it has become. These companies need their audience to be idle. They want them to sit still for long hours and steadily consume the processed foods advertised on television. (*5 Support Sentences*)

Instead of uplifting and improving society, television has had the opposite effect. (*Topic Sentence*) Most opportunities to educate people are passed over for the chance to shock or offend. The time for reading, conversing, and taking meals together as a family has been usurped in many homes by television viewing. While viewing, people are encouraged to eat less-than-healthful foods and discouraged from stirring any distance from the television screen. Television has done little or nothing to advance the education, health, or welfare of people in our society today. (*Concluding Sentence*)

I assure you that this 350-word, 1-3-1 essay really did almost write itself. The actual process of writing it took less than 20 minutes, since I was only writing a more formal version of my freewriting notes.

The contextual thinking, including freewriting, sorting, and thinking about how to order the ideas on my individual notes, took a lot less than 20 minutes. The system works, even though the essay did come out as a rather strong condemnation of TV, which was not my idea going in. This method will permit you to develop an opinion based on evidence, not emotion, and the examiners will see it that way and reward you.

ONE MORE TIME

Let's try one more essay. I will begin the process and take it through the first three steps, but then you write the essay. Here is the topic: *Standardizing attire in schools is beneficial to students, school, and society. Agree or disagree.*

The first thing that springs to my mind is that "standardizing attire" is another way of saying "dress code." So I wrote that thought down. (Don't wait for the freewriting phase. If a good idea occurs to you, write it down.)

1. Contextual Thinking. As always, think in context by first asking what the subject of the sentence—attire—is a part of. I did.

This one is not as simple as the television example. However, a quick look at the dictionary told me that the fact that we humans dress or clothe our bodies is due to the fact that it is a custom or a tradition. Apparently, our practice of clothing ourselves is a part of a greater and less specific category further up the hierarchy that we can call "Tradition" or "Custom."

Diagram I

```
┌─────────────────┐
│ Traditon/Custom │
└─────────────────┘
         │
     ┌───────┐
     │ Attire │
     └───────┘
```

The next question is: What other categories does it make sense to include as the other parts of tradition and custom? What sprang to my mind were manners, laws, ethics, and worship. These came to mind because a custom or tradition is something—let's call it a practice—to which we humans have habitually clung since the dawn of civilization. Oh! That brings another idea to mind. Why did we first put on clothes, or develop laws, or come up with a code of behavior toward one another, or standardize forms of worship? That's for you to ponder and certainly makes excellent fodder for an essay.

Diagram J

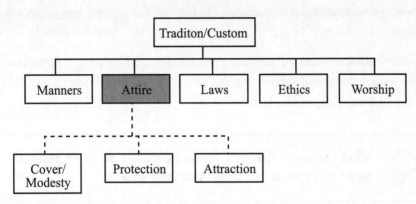

One thing is certain from this contextual exercise, and that is that the idea of dress or apparel is on a par with some pretty lofty human endeavors. In context, we see that dressing ourselves is part of the long process of development of the human race.

One of the wonderful outcomes of contextual thinking is that you never know where it might lead. One of the most valuable lessons of contextual thinking is that it makes sense not to decide on a thesis or point of view until you have looked at the painting from a distance first. As a result, your mind is open to many possibilities. This is the source of your creativity!

2. Constituent Parts. Now that we have looked at our subject—attire—from a few "giant steps" back, so to speak, we can go ahead and put it under the microscope to examine what it is made of. Refer to the boxes beneath Attire in Diagram J above to see this.

It seemed to me that clothes have three distinct purposes. Your ideas may vary. To me, the first purpose of clothing is for cover or modesty, an endeavor that probably first was accomplished using vegetation, animal skins, or animal hair. Of course, this raises the question of why we felt obliged, all those tens of thousands of years ago, to cover our bodies at all. Perhaps it was the introduction of new, unrelated members of our species, or perhaps it was that we moved out of Africa and it was simply cold, which leads to the second purpose: protection against weather. Third, clothes soon moved beyond a utilitarian purpose and began to be used to make us more attractive.

One endearing fact of humanity is that we like to please ourselves; our clothes reflect this and establish our individuality. Only secondarily do we seem to dress to attract the opposite sex.

 All of the above thoughts should be written down on separate pieces of paper or self-stick removable notes.

3. Turn the Topic into a Question. Turn the essay topic into a question. Would standardized dress benefit students, schools, and society?

Now is the time to freewrite. At this stage, there are no bad ideas—just ideas. I did some freewriting and came up with the following. You may add to this list with thoughts that the first two steps have provoked.

> Dress code is a way to make people conform, such as in the military or in a team sport, where the benefits are obvious. No one wants to shoot at someone on the same side or pass the ball to the opposition.

> Clothes are important in that they help us cope with climate.

> Clothes are important because they cover the body parts we want covered.

> One form of dress code could be total nudity; it's cheap and easy to enforce. Just joking.

> Who decides on the standards?

> Is a dress code a form of coercion?

> Is enforcing a dress code legal?

> Is the cost to parents more or less?

> It eliminates "What will I wear today?" issues.

➤ A uniform can become a source of pride and identity, as well as a rallying point.

➤ Clothing is a form of disguise.

➤ Clothes can be formal or informal.

➤ Two vital attributes of clothing are comfort and appearance.

➤ Clothing is a form of personal expression and individuality. Are there others? Hair, jewelry, mannerisms?

➤ Individuality during high school years is important.

➤ Individuality during high school years leaves richer students at an advantage.

➤ Individuality leads to cliques or, worse, gangs.

➤ There are other, less dangerous, ways to express individuality.

 Do you think that I could have come up with this list of 18 issues, conjectures, thoughts, and ideas if I had simply started to write without the preparation outlined in the above steps?

Now, write each point, plus any others you can think of, as notes and sort them into categories. A first category might be arguments for and against the proposition. Perhaps you might want to eliminate some ideas. In any event, you now have the skeleton of your essay. In later chapters, we will discuss ways to make the transitions from one paragraph to another seamless.

4. Write. Right now, before reading the next chapters, pick one side or another on the issue of having a dress code for schools and write a thesis (point of view) statement that makes your position clear and hints at what arguments you will use to prove your point. Now write a 1-3-1, 250- to 350-word essay.

Your Essay

_____

_____

_____

_____

_____

_____

_____

_____

_____

_____

_____

_____

_____

_____

_____

_____

_____

_____

_____

_____

_____

_____

If you are using this book independently, be sure to discuss how you followed the techniques in the first three steps above with a parent, teacher, counselor, or friend, and be very tough on yourself.

Here is another sample topic: *Civilized conduct makes good sense. Agree or disagree.*

These are the steps I took—and the notes I wrote—in order to develop an opinion on the subject:

In thinking about the word "civility," which is what civilized conduct really means, I thought about what civility is a part of. The answer, of course, is that it is part of acceptable social behavior. And acceptable social behavior is, in turn, part of the general code of conduct expected of all human beings, as part of the price for living in a civilized society. The phrase "civilized society" seems redundant; in order to be classified as a society, it must be civilized. That thought is a good candidate for an opening sentence, I thought, and noted it down.

On the next page, you can see what I had discovered so far.

Diagram K

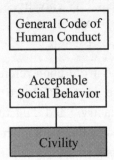

It seems to me that there are two types of codes of conduct. There are the rules that society makes up and to which we are all expected to adhere if we wish to participate in social exchanges, and there are those seemingly innate rules that obey the dictates of our conscience. These latter rules are not man-made—or are they? (This idea could be the subject of another essay: "Where does our conscience originate?")

So I can now proceed to add to the previous diagram, as follows:

Diagram L

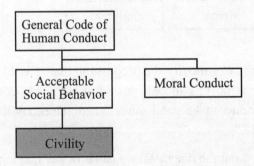

Next, I consulted my dictionaries and a thesaurus in order to further examine the main word in this exercise, "civility." This is an exercise that always bears fruit. You will never, ever be short of ideas if you read definitions of words and look up similar, alternative words (synonyms). I have also found it useful to look up antonyms; they, too, will prompt ideas.

This is a partial list of synonyms for the word "civility": "politeness," "graciousness," "respectfulness," "chivalry," "gallantry," "gentlemanly behavior," "ladylike behavior," "savoir-faire," "unctuousness," "suaveness," "glibness," and "oily and honeyed words."

I hope that you noticed, as I did upon referencing the last five synonyms and near-synonyms, that there is a difference between "graciousness" and "glibness" and between "gallantry" and "unctuousness." The difference is *sincerity*; and therein lies an interesting paragraph—civility can be genuine, and it can also be an insidious subterfuge. So, now look at Diagram M.

Diagram M

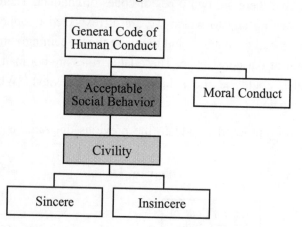

So now we can qualify or modify the proposition that "Civilized conduct makes good sense." We can do this by asking and answering a couple of questions: "Does civilized conduct make good sense?" and "Does civilized conduct make sense for everyone?"

Having worked out the diagrams, we can now see that a good starting point might be to state that only sincere civilized behavior can be good for all of society. This, of course, leads to a problem (and another good point of discussion in the essay): Who are the truly gallant ones, and who are only seemingly gallant—those whose behavior is really unctuous, empty, self-serving, hollow, disingenuous, pretentious, artificial, dishonest, and downright oily? How can we know the difference?

Who, What, Why, Where, and When? It always helps to ask these questions about the topic in question. For example,

Who benefits from civilized conduct?

What is civilized behavior?

Why is civilized behavior important?

Where is civilized behavior necessary?

When is it important to behave in a civilized manner?

Always remember to personalize the topic by asking how important civilized behavior is to me, my family, my community, my country, and the world. Note specific examples whenever possible in your responses.

Having written ideas on pieces of paper and categorized the ideas, it is time to decide on a **thesis.** Remember that the thesis is your **point of view,** your **opinion,** and sometimes it is called the **controlling idea** of the essay.

The thesis sentence (or sentences) opens the first paragraph of the essay. It should state your opinion on the topic clearly, and it should suggest some of the thoughts that you will expound upon in the later—body or support—paragraphs. The last paragraph is where you wrap things up.

Here are three options for opening (thesis) sentences.

"The very essence of a civilized society is to be found in the conduct of its members toward one another. (*Thesis*) In fact, a perfectly civilized society would have no need of laws, for citizens would know how to behave in a manner that helped society flourish." (*Seed*)

"Courtesy, or civilized conduct, is to society what lubricants are to a machine. (*Thesis*) Civil society is a machine and will work better if friction between its parts is eliminated." (*Seed*)

"Civility," "civil," "civilian," "civic," and "civilization" are all words rooted in the Latin word for citizen, which was intended to mean a person of good conduct. It seems to me that the Romans, and the Greeks, from whom the Romans borrowed this idea, intended to base civil order on trust. (*Thesis*) Some personal responsibility for the common good must be borne by everyone; civilizations fail when a few powerful individuals ignore the common good." (*Seed*)

I have chosen to use the second example to expand into an essay. As you know, the format for essays in this book is the 250- to 350-word essay, which has five, roughly equal paragraphs.

As an aside, some students I worked with in preparing this book asked me why they should be confined to this format. It is too limiting, they said. My answer is simple. Artists choose the size of a canvas to be appropriate to their subject. The edges or borders of their canvas set a limit, albeit an artificial one, so there is no painting where the viewer does not expect any. If a poet decides to write in iambic pentameter or if a playwright chooses verse and a novelist prose, then that too is their limitation. Is it not also their opportunity to excel in the medium they have chosen? Byron, Shakespeare, and Dickens did quite well while not straying from their self-imposed constraints.

Here is the essay.

essay

Civilized conduct makes good sense. Agree or disagree.

Courtesy is to society what lubricants are to a machine. Civil society is a machine and will work better if friction between its parts is eliminated. History tells us that eliminating friction between people or between human institutions is not possible, so the goal should be more modest. Machinery lubricants, after all, do not come close to eliminating friction; they simply work to minimize it.

Friction in nature causes heat. Racing cars, boats, and spacecraft all try to move through or over their medium, whether it is air, water, or terra firma, with the minimum of resistance. They do this by paying attention to design and by using lubricants. Lubricants in an engine act as a balm or a salve, they prevent wear and tear, perhaps they even heal and renew. Whatever else they do, they prolong the useful life of the engine or machine. Friction between humans and between the institutions they create also causes heat—emotional heat. Emotional heat causes conflict, and conflict all too frequently results in death, injury, or at least court cases. How much of this could be avoided if we all just got along?

The late comedian Rodney Dangerfield often used a line about not getting any respect. In other words, people disrespected him: they were discourteous, uncivil, and impolite. He was, of course, making fun of this behavior, but the sad truth is that, according to a respected survey firm, almost 80 percent of company employees feel that they, too, get little or no respect. If that is true in the workplace, then it is almost certainly true in schools and even families.

Most of us feel angered by being forced to listen to one side of a cell phone conversation or by the sound of a car masquerading as a disco sound system on wheels. Does that cause heat? Does the other person's inconsiderate behavior help move us toward a frictionless society? Or, could we all learn that someone's right to occupy a space ends at other people's ears or noses or eyes?

I think that we are all better off in learning, earning, or family settings when less heat is given off. Incivility is detrimental to all of our health and well-being. The reverse of this is that we would all learn, earn, and smile more if people would just be a little more gallant. Society, like an engine, is made up of moving parts, after all.

The **main lesson** to take away from this exercise is not my essay, but **the process** by which the essay was developed. Learn this, and you will be able to discover a point of view on almost anything and to disclose it in well-ordered, convincing prose. And, by the way, you will also find out more about the most important topic of all: **you.**

Here are some more essay topics for you: *Beauty is only skin deep*; *Honesty is the best policy*; *Combating pollution through environmentalism is the world's greatest challenge*; *Prisoners have more rights and privileges than law-abiding citizens*. Pick one or more topics and practice, practice, practice!

Oddly, the more philosophical and important the topic, the easier it is to apply these techniques. The more specific the topic—"The School Principal Enjoys a Joke," for example—the harder it is to think in context. However, it is still important to try.

Are you ready for another topic? Here is the prompt: *Money is the Root of All Evil. Discuss.* Now, there is a philosophical subject if ever I saw one. To write an essay on this topic, you will have to think about two of life's more enduring aspects: wickedness and wealth. Let's take a crack at it anyway. First, try *Thinking Around the Box*^{TM}. In fact, this time, think around two boxes. One labeled "Money" and the second one called "Evil." This is not going to be an easy exercise; however, I can assure you that it would be much more difficult to write a good essay on this topic without contextual thinking.

Since schools are not supposed to teach religious belief, I will simply state the obvious—that good and evil are evident parts of our society—in the following diagram.

Diagram N

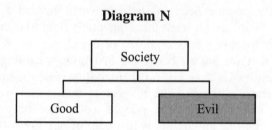

Now draw a box and put the word "Money" inside it. What is it a part of? My answer is "The Economy."

Diagram O

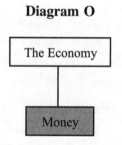

I did some thinking about the word "Economy" and came up with this next chart. Money is a part of our economy, but so are the other items below. Only then did I break down "Money" into its component parts.

Diagram P

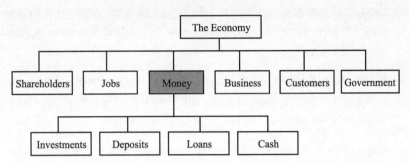

Of course, this exercise in brainstorming prompted the usual crop of ideas, thoughts, and hunches. I wrote them all down as they occurred to me. Here they are:

➤ Evil is the absence of good in our lives and in those of others.

➤ Evil is wickedness.

➤ Evil is the opposite of good.

➤ The result of evil is harm, suffering, and injury.

➤ The signs of evil are anger, spite, malice, hate, envy, and a good many other dreadful but all-too-prevalent symptoms.

➤ Money is the medium of exchange issued by a government.

➤ I couldn't help but think of the Reality TV shows that are based on high rewards and exploitation; encouraging humiliation, malice, spite, greed, and the plotting of others' downfalls. Are they a metaphor for business today? Do employees have to check their values at the door when reporting for a day at the office or factory?

➤ Without the discovery of trade, humans would still be in the Stone Age.

➤ Commerce is one of the engines of discovery. Patronage is another.

➤ Business is Darwinian. Only the fittest employees survive and only the fittest businesses survive. Old businesses are destroyed to make way for newer, more responsive ones. It's called "creative destruction" by economists.

➤ What about fairness in all this? Does the migrant worker deserve better? Should the shareholders and better paid employees give up some of their benefits to help the less fortunate?

➤ Capitalism is based on money. It's certainly not perfect, but, like democracy, it is the best solution we have come up with to date. The twin totalitarian systems—Communism and Fascism—have left misery, strife, and pollution in their wake.

➤ Misuse of power mars business practices.

Now, turn the topic into a question. Is money the root of all evil? Having written all of the above points on separate pieces of paper and sorted them into categories, decide what your point of view is and begin with a thesis statement. Then, write a 1-3-1 essay. Here's an example of how such an essay might turn out:

essay

Money is the root of all evil. Discuss.

Money clearly has the potential to promote evil, but to call it the root of all evil is to give it too much power. Money is really just a medium of exchange. The nature of money's effect on individuals, on a country, on society as a whole depends on how it is regarded, how it is obtained, and how it is used.

If money becomes the sole criterion by which we, as a society, measure our success, then other values will suffer by becoming less esteemed. The health, education, and welfare of our citizens is less than important if only money matters. There is, then, no argument for spending money on the protection of children, humanitarian aid in response to a crisis, or public safety, if that spending would reduce our store of "success." The worship of money can justify all sorts of wicked behavior and trample the values that help keep us in balance.

Is business to be based, like "reality" television shows, on high monetary rewards through exploitation—encouraging humiliation, malice, spite, greed, and the plotting of others' downfalls? If so, obtaining money becomes an invitation to evil, causing harm, suffering, and injury to most of the "players." But, if business is based on honesty, integrity, and rules of fair play, then obtaining money can also become a means of service and fulfillment for business people and others.

How is money to be used? Clearly, it can be spent, saved, or invested, on behalf of oneself or others—for good or evil. In general, society claims a portion of money earned for taxes, which are intended to be spent on the common welfare. The use of the rest is subject (beyond the amounts needed to keep anything from a household to a major corporation "in business") to the character of the individuals and businesses controlling it.

Money is neither good nor evil, but it may promote either. It's a question of extremes. If it becomes too important (in and of itself), if getting it is based on "no holds barred," and if it used selfishly, cruelly, spitefully, evil follows. As a value among values, obtained with honesty and integrity and used wisely in a spirit of service, money can do great good. Like most other things in life, balance is the key.

SHORTCUT METHODS

Perhaps because of limited time or the fact that the topic is quite specific, contextual thinking with diagramming and freewriting may not be the ideal approach. You might want to employ a related method that is simpler and faster and still helps with the first task when writing an essay, namely *discovery*.

Spider Diagrams

This first shortcut works well with serious topics, especially if you are visually oriented and like to see the organization of your ideas. This method is primarily a variation on the diagramming portion of contextual thinking.

Spider diagrams work like this: Write the topic you are concerned with in the middle of a page. Draw a box around it. Now draw four more boxes for primary ideas to the northwest, northeast, southwest, and southeast of your first circle. You can add boxes as more thoughts occur to you. Let's say it is the television topic again. First, put the initials "TV" in a box as in Diagram Q below, and then begin the process of thinking about it diagrammatically.

Diagram Q

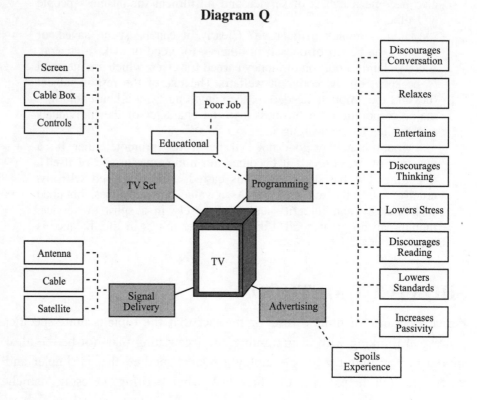

The TV topic evokes four primary ideas:

1. Programming

2. The TV set itself

3. Advertising

4. Delivery of the TV signal

These four ideas, in turn, encourage other ideas that are subsets of the first four.

Now, pick one of these primary ideas and think about ideas you get from that primary idea. In the space provided, draw as many boxes as you have ideas relating to it. Soon, you will have a complete Spider Diagram, with ideas to help you form an opinion and also provide paragraph topics. Your ideas are already categorized—you will find your topics in the boxes that are connected to the primary ideas in your diagram.

Your Spider Diagram

Topics best suited for a Spider Diagram may also benefit from a more detailed exploration when time is not an issue. Following are a couple of examples.

Let's use the following prompt as our first example: *In a popular TV commercial for a camera, a famous tennis star says, "Image is everything." Is he right?*

I decided to use the Spider Diagram approach, since the proposition suggested by the essay topic is quite straightforward. Here is how I addressed the issue. Thinking about this statement, I realized that there are only two significant words in it. One of them is the word "image," which needs to be explored in detail. The other significant word is "everything," which needs no further explanation.

In referring to the dictionary and thesaurus, I came up with a list of words that allowed me to explore the word "image" and the issues suggested by its usage. Here they are: "duplication," "representative forms," "a replica," "a personification (as in "she is the image of health")," and "a personality and character, deliberately projected to the public."

Next, I posed the topic as a question. Is *image* everything? My instinctive response to this question was, of course, no. However, it always helps to refrain from making a determination until the full exploration process is complete. So I asked myself the following Who?, What?, Why?, Where?, and When? questions:

Q. Who is affected by images?

A. Who is not affected?

Q. What are images?

A. They are duplicates, representations, replicas, facsimiles, copies, resemblances.

Q. Why do images exist?

A. First and foremost, images exist because humans can make images. They also help us to remember, to communicate, to fool people, to describe scenes and people, and to act as visual metaphors.

Q. Where do images exist?

A. They exist everywhere—even in a cave with only fire to cast shadows as ghostly images of life. Use a search engine to look up "Plato's Cave" and enjoy his use of images as metaphors.

Q. When do we see images?

A. We see images when our eyes are open, and, intriguingly, also when our eyes are closed.

As usual, it helps to personalize the issue and ask how images affect us, our families, and our nation. Concrete examples are very desirable, and using a Spider Diagram has the advantage of categorizing the ideas while constructing the diagram.

Diagram R

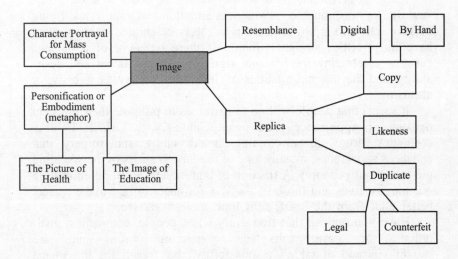

Here is the essay.

essay

In a popular TV commercial for a camera, a famous tennis star says, "Image is everything." Is he right?

Image is not everything—there is more to life than facsimiles of things. However, in this age of celebrity and mass communications, "image" is close to being the sum total of the message we are fed on a daily basis. We are led to believe that appearance is indeed everything. (*Thesis*) Sneakers that send the "right message" about the wearer now cost more than a week's groceries. (*Seed*) Plastic surgery and steroid usage are almost epidemics in the western world. (*Seed*) The promotion and maintenance of the image, or public persona, of companies, institutions, people, and even our own government, has become more important than their substance. (*Seed*) The problem is that images frequently lie.

The first thing we see when we encounter a person is their form or appearance. Sadly, the very first things we notice are the superficialities: clothing, cosmetics, hair, shape, gender, color, handicaps, and size. It is true that these external factors will tell us a great deal about that person. Nevertheless, in order to further examine the person, we need more. We need to know what the other dimension—the invisible one—is composed of.

Image is celebrated as never before. To be "cool," "sexy," "in," "trendy," or "fashionable" is to attract attention and gain status. Being diligent, clever, kind, or courteous is rarely celebrated. Does society have its priorities straight? Shouldn't there be more of a balance between celebrating the external signs of physical talent and desirability, and the internal qualities of, let's say, bravery, generosity, or altruism?

It seems that people will go to extremes to promote their physical persona or appearance. The beauty industry, in which I lump cosmetics, drugs, diets, clothing, health clubs, and surgery that enhances appearance, must be one of the largest slices of the spending pie that is our economy. A fraction of that money, spent on enhancing our interior lives and those of the less fortunate, might make us feel better and (from the inside out) look more attractive.

Have you noticed that frequently when people, companies, institutions, or governments do something wrong—and are caught—instead of taking responsibility, they reach for the image repair specialists who apply their expertise to "spin" the situation favorably? A simple apology might save our economy a great deal of money; of course, we would all have to look elsewhere for entertainment. Then again, I might be making far too much of the clever comparison that the TV commercial was making between the image of a tennis star and the fact that the purpose of cameras is to make images.

Now that I'm down off my soapbox, did you notice the mistake in the fourth sentence of the second paragraph? Microsoft Word did. "To further examine" is a split infinitive, and to strict grammarians and editors, this is a "no-no."

You, of course, might explore and examine the topic regarding the word "image," and discover, and disclose, a completely different conclusion. That would be absolutely valid. The important lesson to be learned is that it is vital to use a process or system, such as the one this book describes, by which you can come to a point of view that is well thought out, logical, authentic, and arguable in an essay.

You might not condone the way I approached the issue, or the conclusions I drew in the last essay—or in any of the essays in the book—but you probably agree that they would stand out in the minds of examiners or admissions directors who are searching for those authentic, original voices that do stand out. Make sure yours is one of them.

Holding a different opinion is not intrinsically right or wrong. It is an opinion's authenticity that matters. In other words, if the conclusion was arrived at using a well-thought-out, systematic method, then the reader knows that you are capable of original thought; and that's what counts.

Here is a new prompt for another example: *One of the main goals of an American high school is to prepare its students for the role of good citizen. How are you and your school measuring up?*

This topic also lends itself to the Spider Diagram approach. As you prepare the diagram, remember to get definitions first, look at alternative words, note thoughts on the subject, answer the Who?, What?, Why?, Where?, and When? questions, personalize the topic, include concrete examples, and write. Remember also to polish and edit (see Chapters 6 and 7).

All the definitions I discovered for "citizen" or "citizenship" had to do with a form of membership in a country and with the associated rights, privileges, and obligations that go with that membership. Of course, citizenship is a very different category of membership than membership in, say, a health club. It is, however, a membership because it is exclusive.

The best definition I found was by a former Supreme Court justice from the 1950s named Warren Harding, who said that "Citizenship is a person's basic right, because it is our right to have rights."

Other words that have the same or similar meanings are: "countrymen," "inhabitants," "populace," "settler," and "colonist." A good exercise might be to look up the antonyms of "citizen." Once you see words like "serf" and "slave," you probably will get some ideas. The root of the word "citizen" is Latin and then French (which is mostly Latin) and it means "city." High schools tend to teach the art of citizenship in the civics class. Another way of saying civics is "political science."

Now, I turned the topic into a question—in this case, a new question. "Is it clear that one of my school's goals is to make me a good citizen?" The Who?, What?, Why?, Where?, and When? questions came next:

Q. Who is affected by the idea of or the conferring of citizenship?

A. All citizens are affected, of course, but so are those who are not citizens and, as a result, do not have the same rights, protections, and obligations.

Q. What is citizenship?

A. Citizenship is the right to have the rights of being a citizen.

Q. Why is citizenship important?

A. This is a very good question, and one that is at the heart of the essay topic. Without an agreement by all the citizens on why it is important to be citizens, with the same rights and privileges and obligations, anarchy would prevail. If no one living in a named country that was recognized by all the other countries had any obligations or rights or privileges, then there would be no laws to protect them.

Q. Where can one be a citizen?

A. Can a holder of a passport from a country that is not truly democratic be considered a citizen?

Q. When can one be a citizen?

A. The answer here seems to be somewhat ambiguous. If you cannot vote, are you a full citizen, or just an underprivileged one? If you are legally a resident in a country, paying taxes, performing military service, and abiding by the law, can you—or should you—be considered a citizen? Are there classes of citizenship? Should there be classes of citizenship?

Personalizing an issue by asking what it means to you and your neighbors is always a good idea, as is noting concrete examples whenever possible. For the most part, categorization occurs as the ideas are worked into the Spider Diagram.

Take a look at Diagram S on the following page to see what I came up with.

Diagram S

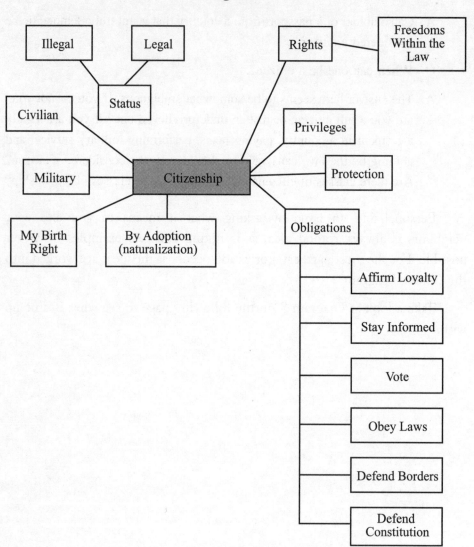

Here is the essay.

essay

One of the main goals of an American high school is to prepare its students for the role of good citizen. How are you and your school measuring up?

No one disputes the fact that the USA is the only superpower in the world today. In a sense, to be a citizen of the USA is like being a citizen of other superpowers in history: it is a great privilege. The difference between us and the other historical superpowers, such as the ancient Persians and Romans or the British in the sixteenth to nineteenth centuries, is that we, the people, are all to be seen as created equal and treated equitably. This is our strength. Our citizens are equal under the law. In Persia, Rome, and Britain, some were more equal than others were. Our schools are supposed to teach us this lesson, and mine does. I feel prepared for the day when I will vote, because I have studied not only American history, but the history of other societies also. (*This last sentence is the thesis sentence of the essay and includes the seeds of ideas, which will be developed later. You should note that it is perfectly fine to write the thesis—or point of view or controlling idea—at the end of the first paragraph.*)

An elite band of Roman aristocrats led their empire's growth with a combination of military, engineering, and administrative skills. They believed that citizenship had to be earned. Sadly, however, it could also be bought. Citizenship was not available to all in the society, which was built in tiers, with slaves at the bottom. It never recognized the contributions of women, but it was good at recognizing the skills of some of the elites in their conquered lands.

The genius of our founding fathers was that they believed in the French revolutionary ideals of liberty, fraternity, and equality—qualities that the French soon forgot and, consequently, returned to dictatorship after a brief period of freedom. No Napoleon or Lenin appeared in the USA to steal the revolution. The stains on the reputation of our founding fathers were to exclude the slave population and the indigenous, native peoples from the table, going so far as to make them legally worth a mere fraction of a white man, and to exclude women from civic participation.

The 1860s saw a war that was fought to remedy this execrable situation and the 1960s saw brave leaders enact the remedy into laws of civil rights. It has taken almost fifty years for many to catch up to the idea that all must breathe the same air and walk the same earth. Our strength lies in the fact that we are doing this.

This is what I have learned at my high school, and I feel strongly that this has prepared me to participate in the world's best—and, to my mind, the only true—democracy.

Lists

This second shortcut works well with less serious topics. You may particularly enjoy this method if you are primarily verbal in your approach to ideas. This method is a variation on the freewriting portion of contextual thinking.

To use this method, you build lists of thoughts, conjectures, and comments on the subject. (If time is not a problem, you may wish to get definitions and related words, answer the Who?, What?, Why?, Where?, and When? questions, personalize the topic, and include examples.) You use the lists to begin discovering your point of view and getting ideas for paragraphs and sentences that support it. Let's say that the topic to be written about is: *The value that we put on gardens.*

First, write down as many ideas as possible, and then group them into categories such as recreation/hobby, types of gardens, ingredients, and so on. It always helps to put the statement in the form of a question: Do we put a value on gardens? (A trip to any house and garden store on a Saturday in early Spring will answer this question.)

Once you have done this, it is time to examine your work and decide on a thesis statement about the topic *The value that we put on gardens.* Then, list the proofs for the validity of your point of view, as expressed in the thesis statement, from among your other ideas. I wrote down as many ideas as came to me in a few minutes:

➤ Well-tended gardens enhance houses, in terms of both visual appeal and monetary value.

➤ Gardening as a hobby; working with the soil/nature/weather/plants is satisfying/relaxing/different.

➤ Public and private gardens offer the same advantages to the people who tend them or visit them.

➤ Gardens are not restricted to decorative efforts; they can also supply food.

➤ Gardens require that we manipulate nature. Besides water, fertilizer and insect control are required, and these may be toxic. The introduction of nonnative plants can also be harmful.

I grouped these ideas under three headings: Aesthetic (having to do with a sense of beauty), Practical (useful), and Ecological. I looked at the lists and made a stab at a thesis statement by asking myself what this list indicated to me.

Here it is: *"The proliferation of public and private gardens suggests that we humans have an innate need to control nature, however, we need to do so responsibly."*

See how well you and a group of friends or family members can take this sentence and develop it into a five-paragraph essay, supporting the point of view illustrated in the thesis sentence.

In Chapter 11, there is a section illustrating how contextual thinking (with diagramming and freewriting), spider diagrams, and lists can be applied to topics in order to generate ideas and think your way to an opinion on the subject. Practicing all of these methods in groups, and then alone, will make you view things differently.

Use the space on the following pages for your essay.

Your Essay

_____

_____

_____

_____

_____

_____

_____

_____

_____

_____

_____

_____

_____

_____

_____

_____

_____

_____

_____

_____

FREEWRITING REVISITED

Freewriting really has two parts to it. First, there is the part where ideas just spontaneously occur to you as you carefully examine the topic or prompt. I cannot stress enough how important it is to capture these ideas as they occur. Do this on separate pieces of paper. Blurt them out.

The second part of freewriting is more formal. It consists of a series of routines that you should learn by heart.

Let's say that you have been asked to write an essay on the topic *Honesty is the best policy*. Thoughts will occur spontaneously to you as you contemplate this old proverb. However, there are ways that you can learn to examine the issue and encourage more ideas.

1. Turn the statement into questions: Is honesty always the best way forward? Is there ever a case where honesty is actually a bad idea? Dishonesty seems to work in many walks of life, such as political campaigns—why is that?

2. Who?, What?, Why?, Where?, and When?—apply these words to the prompt or topic. **Who** decides what is honest and not? You, your family, your religion, your government? **What** is honesty? **What** is the opposite of honesty? **What** does it mean to be honest? **Why** is honesty the *best* policy? **Where** does the idea of honesty come from? **When** does it pay to be honest and when does it not pay?

3. Personalize the topic by asking yourself what is your personal stake in this issue. What were the consequences to me, my family, or my community of honest or dishonest conduct by either a family member, a community member, or someone from outside of these groups?

4. Investigate the consequences of honesty or dishonesty by thinking of examples. This is a particularly good idea if you decide to write an essay with stories as examples to prove your point.

5. Find the gaps in your knowledge and don't address any of your weaknesses in your writing. It is good to know what to avoid.

By now, you have used contextual thinking with diagramming and freewriting (or a related shortcut method) to discover and capture a lot of data on the subject about which you have to write. The next step is to decide upon, and begin disclosing, your point of view, by writing your thesis sentence.

This is best achieved by categorizing the ideas and thoughts that you have discovered. As I have advised before, put the notes into an order, such as "Y—supports the proposition" or "N—does not support the proposition." Note that if you have used a Spider Diagram, your ideas are already categorized.

Now write a preliminary thesis statement based on your rereading of your notes. Check that your thesis has a good base of support. That is, do you have a sufficient number of ideas to complete three or more paragraphs supporting your belief?

Then write, rewrite, and polish (See Chapters 6 and 7). Remember to always leave your best piece of evidence until last—where it will have the greatest impact on the reader.

The more you adopt and practice this method of discovery and disclosure, with time devoted to all the segments I have described, the easier it will become. This is why you MUST practice writing essays a great deal. You must practice until the process becomes second nature.

In Short

1. Diagram the topic by putting it into a box and then thinking carefully around it.

2. Write down your thoughts as you do.

3. Now break down the topic itself.

4. Again, write down your thoughts.

(When limited time or the nature of a topic makes numbers 1 to 4 above impractical, a related shortcut method may be used.)

5. Sort your ideas into groupings that agree and that become the basis for paragraphs and topic and support sentences.

6. Write.

Following this method, you will have examined a topic logically and come to an authentic conclusion that also happens to have good supporting evidence.

CHAPTER FIVE

Essay Types, Techniques, and Tone

You need to know that there are two different types of essays and eight different techniques that you can use in writing your essay. It is vital for you to understand that the tone of your essay has implications for your reader. The particular type, techniques, and tone you use create the "voice" the reader of your essay "hears."

TYPES OF ESSAYS

The type of essay that you decide to use is determined by your intent. Do you wish to simply inform your readers, or do you wish to persuade them of the validity of your argument? In either case, you must remember that the purpose of an essay is to express your opinion.

1. **Informative Essays**

   This type of essay is also sometimes called the Expository Essay. It explains something to the reader. A TV documentary on the nocturnal life of lions on the African Savannah is an informative essay, it just happens also to have pictures of the subject. It usually employs the narration technique; more on that in the "Essay Techniques" section of this chapter.

2. **Persuasive Essays**

   These types of essays are also called Argument Essays. Think about what a politician's goal always is—to persuade an audience of the correctness of his or her position—and you will always remember the intent of this type of essay. Much more on how to write an argument essay follows.

ESSAY TECHNIQUES

All of the following essay techniques can be used to support your thesis, or point of view. You may use more than one in an essay.

Illustration. In everyday speech, we often say "for instance" or "for example." What invariably follows these words is an illustration. If you are trying to explain to your grandfather how a computer works, you might begin by comparing the computer to a human being. "For example, Granddad, a computer thinks rather like a person, but instead of talking to tell us what it has done, the monitor or the printer spells it out for us." This is what is meant by illustration. If you wish to explain how a mathematical principle works, it helps to use an illustration. How could you explain compound interest on a loan without using an example?

Narration. In a narrative essay, you recount a series of events in the order in which they occurred (chronologically). "I particularly remember my first day of high school. It was the beginning of a time in my life when I learned to trust people." Obviously, a narrative is going to follow. Incidents will be described that support the writer's main thesis that high school helped him overcome his mistrust of strangers. Of course, all the events must be relevant and support the point. The narrative essay should always be written in the first person, using "I."

"I remember well going to baseball games with my grandfather. It was during these trips that I learned what it meant to serve my country." This is the beginning of a narrative essay and a little exaggeration for the purpose of literary effect is expected; but don't use too much. Incidentally, do not write a narrative essay unless you are really confident of your storytelling abilities.

Description. This method of writing tests your powers of observation. Do you observe your surroundings when you are in class, at the movies, at home, in the supermarket, or at the mall? Can you write down the details, and then can you describe them in such a way that your reader will see them as you did?

What appealed to your five senses at the ballpark that time when you accompanied your grandfather? Did he have the smell of tobacco on his breath? What did the cold drink taste like? What did it feel like to catch the foul ball? What were the most memorable sounds of that game? Most of all, what did the scene look like?

 Try the following exercise. Observe an apple, animal, tree, or plant for a long time and ask yourself about the sensory details: the look, the smell, the feel, and perhaps the sound and taste. What makes them unique? What words come to mind? What thoughts come to mind? Also observe the facts: the color of the apple, the texture of the animal's fur. Was it sunny outside? Then, use the space on the following page to write everything down from memory.

Your Observations

Process Analysis. This is really a descriptive essay, but you are describing a method of doing something correctly. If you have done it well, your readers will be able to duplicate the process. It focuses on the *how*, not the *what*.

If you were writing a narrative essay about the time you helped in a soup kitchen, you would focus on the events of the day, in the order in which they occurred, including lessons learned from the experience. The same essay written purely to describe the process would be more of a guide on how best to accomplish feeding the homeless, without describing the significance of the experience.

Categorization. If you went to the library and asked for a history book, the librarian would not send you to the fiction section or tell you that the books were sorted by size or color. The librarian would know where to send you because the library's collection is categorized, or cataloged.

If you are using examples to demonstrate a point, organize them into categories. In the example above, where you and your grandfather sat at the ballpark and discussed what it means to serve one's country, it makes sense to organize all his examples of service into categories. He may have served in the military; that's one category. He may have become a politician after leaving the service; that's another category. His brother may have joined the Peace Corps, and his son, the Diplomatic Service. Keeping the categories together improves the essay.

Definition. Let's say that you have to write an essay that deals with honesty. A good way to start is by defining the word: "Honesty means being truthful" or "Honesty means integrity." You can also define it by stating what it is not: "Being honest means not lying."

As an exercise, try selecting a few words such as "crime," "disease," "sportsmanship," and "personality," and defining them. It helps to ask yourself a few questions about the word, on topics such as why the word is important, what the word means, and how important the word is. Use the following pages for this.

Your Definitions

Your Definitions

Your Definitions

Comparison and Contrast. To compare is to show similarities and differences. To contrast is to show only the differences.

"Both of the universities I am interested in offer undergraduate degrees in computer science. There the similarities end, however. One university is large; the other is small. One is on the East Coast; the other is in the Midwest. One dates back to pre-Revolutionary times; the other was founded in 1943."

You can compare one thing with another in your essay, pointing out both similarities and differences. You can also exclusively contrast one thing with another. Comparison, in particular, is an excellent literary device; it helps to bring your reader into your world.

Argument, or Statement and Proof. Argument in this context does not mean to quarrel, fight, or disagree. It means a course of reasoning using facts, evidence, and logic intended to demonstrate the truth or falsehood of a position. Whole books have been written on this subject. What you need to know follows.

More than 2,300 years ago, Aristotle stripped the argument down to its bare bones: "First, state a thing to be true. Second, prove it." Your goal is to persuade your audience to accept your stated thesis.

Be careful, though, because some things do not need to be proved. They are not debatable. You do not want to spend an hour proving that coal and oil are the main sources of energy in America. This is not a debatable statement. It is not controversial in the sense that it is a fact. It is only controversial in that it may not be the wisest policy to use coal and oil as the main energy sources.

An argument essay is built around a **specific thesis** or point of view that claims something that you believe in and are prepared to defend. For example, "Alternative sources of energy, such as wind and solar, must be developed to meet America's energy needs in the twenty-first century."

Make sure that your claim is not **vague.** "Alternative energy sources must be found." This thesis statement is so vague that it is neither debatable nor controversial. Worst of all, it is boring.

How do you prove your case? You prove it by **logic** and **evidence.**

Logic

Logic can be a devastating way to advance and prove your point. I can think of three general types of logical argument:

1. A cause-and-effect argument can show your audience that you know how to think things through. You demonstrate that "Cause A" leads to "Effect B," and you further show how "Effect B" can result in "Effect C," which leads to "Effect D."

   On the issue of alternative energy sources, the cause-and-effect logic might look like this:

   > Alternative sources of energy, such as wind and solar, must be developed and put to use soon (*Thesis*) because our dependence on foreign oil (*Cause A*) is leading to political instability in the world (*Effect B*). Wars and pricing problems have an unfair effect on our lower income citizens (*Effect C*). As a result the citizens who can least afford it are going to be hurt the most (*Effect D*).
   > Can you think of an Effect E?

2. I like to outline this sort of logical argument in the following shorthand: *A should do B because of C.*

   > "Students should all study essay writing because it is now a mandatory part of the SAT and an optional part of the ACT Assessment." In this case, students are A. The action—studying essay writing—is B. The reason, which is C, is that essays are now part of these important tests. (This sort of argument only works, of course, if C is a compelling reason.)

3. The third arrow in the logical quiver is the argument I referred to as syllogistic logic, back in Chapter 2. If A is true or non-debatable, such as "All human beings are mortal," and if B is also true—and related—such as "I am a human being," then C can be concluded or deduced: "I am mortal." Always make sure that the two premises (A and B) are related; otherwise, the logic will be flawed, as in the following

example: *Trees have leaves. Geraniums have leaves. Therefore all geraniums are trees.* Geraniums and trees indeed have leaves in common, but they are not related; geraniums are flowers, not trees.

Evidence

Evidence to support your argument comes in the form of facts, statistics, authorities, anecdotes, and scenarios.

Facts. "Importing almost all of our energy is unfair." This is not a fact; it is an opinion that can be defended with facts, such as, "Importing 90 percent of our energy sources has been demonstrated to be strategically dangerous."

Statistics. If you are backing your argument with statistics, make sure that they come from a reliable, authentic source. Encyclopedias and government agencies are reliable; obscure Web sites on the Internet are not.

Authorities. A quote from an authority on the subject you are writing about adds authenticity to your argument.

Anecdotes. A story that is widely acknowledged to be true is a powerful tool to add to your essay.

Fictional Scenarios. A story about an outcome that *could* be true can also help your case. "Imagine if everyone decided to leave charitable contributions to the next guy, and stopped making donations to children's hospitals, disease research and support services groups, and disaster relief funds."

In an argument essay where the topic is controversial, you should remember that there is no right answer, only your opinion on the matter. That is just fine, however, because whoever is judging your essay is only looking for how well you argue your point. In debates, people are regularly asked to defend a position they do not believe. That is good practice for an argument essay.

ESSAY TONE

In conversations, we automatically set a tone that is appropriate to the setting. Even small children do this. You would not speak to a school principal in the same tone of voice that you use to talk to your best friend or your sister. The tone of your voice reflects the moment, the audience, and the message. It is your personality on full display. The same applies in essay composition.

If you are talking on the telephone with a friend and arranging to meet, you might take on a playful tone. If you have been offended, then you might take a righteous or hurtful tone with the person who offended you. We all know the tone of voice that is used in a conversation about a third party who is not present; sadly it is mostly conspiratorial, secretive, or gossipy, and rarely, if ever, praiseworthy. If you are describing a problem you are having, then you probably adopt a serious tone of voice. Sarcasm, irony, pity, and romance are all transmitted through your tone of voice. I would go so far as to say that the tone of your essay is one of the main impressions that a reader will take away.

 Since you are writing essentially about yourself, take great care about the tone you adopt.

Think of the tone you use as reflecting your attitude about the subject you are speaking or writing about. Think of your voice as the outward sign of your personality or your frame of mind. Be aware that any readers of your written work and any listeners to your spoken words become instantly aware of your attitude. This is a fact that you must learn to use to your advantage.

There are two basic tones that you can adopt. One is formal and the other is informal, which is more conversational or intimate. Look at the following five ways of introducing a topic and decide which type is appropriate to both your personality and the topic, and which is suitable to an informal or formal tone.

A Background Statement. "Up until the late 1960s, many people were discriminated against on the basis of skin color, gender, or age." Or, "Honesty is one of the fundamental virtues of a society and is always the best course of action." Both statements set the stage for a formal tone.

A Question. "Are you one of the many people who are unable to fix a car or a faucet?" Or, "Have you ever wondered why honesty is always the best policy?" These questions set the stage for an informal essay.

A Story. "I was 12 before I saw snow for the first time." Or, "When I was 7 or 8, an incident took place that changed my life forever." An informal tone is probably going to follow the first statement and either a formal or informal tone could follow the second, depending on the incident.

A Fact. "In September 2001, the mainland of the United States was invaded for the first time since the founding of the republic." Or, "The prison population recently topped two million inmates. This is a disturbing fact, until one considers that this means that 99.3 percent of Americans are law abiding." A formal tone is appropriate in the first case, of course. In the second case, it depends.

A Definition. "Television service is part of the world wide information distribution system." Or, "Virtue is defined as moral excellence. For many of us, that means honesty—since without honesty, many other virtues, such as patriotism or caregiving, lose their meaning." Formal tones would follow here also, I think.

It is an interesting exercise to frame each of the above examples in another way to see how the tone changes. For example, in the story way of introducing a topic, the first sample introduction reads: "I was 12 before I saw snow for the first time." If you couched this as a fact, it might read "Many 12-year-old children have never seen snow." Try turning the other examples around. It changes the tone radically and sets up a very different essay.

Keep in mind that timidity, vagueness, indecision, evasiveness, and wordiness, or repetitiveness, negatively affect the tone of your essay. Furthermore, never adopt a tone that indicates you are whining. You may have every reason to complain about the issue you are writing about, but be constructive, don't ask for pity. (Nobody likes a whining applicant.) Also avoid both scolding and being pompous, as these tones are sure to disengage your reader. As for denouncing something in bombastic terms—even if you believe what you are writing about with every fiber of your being—don't do it in your SAT, ACT Assessment, or college application essay. Once you are a newspaper columnist or TV commentator, then you can do it.

Finally, again, getting it right means practice. If you are now in grade 11, you should write at least a dozen essays before taking your exams. Don't wait until you are in the examination room to write your first-ever essay—that is a sure way to fail.

In Short

1. An informative essay explains something.

2. A persuasive essay argues your case.

3. You can use illustration as a technique by writing, "For example."

4. You can narrate, "I remember my first day of kindergarten."

5. You can describe an event, "My High School Graduation."

6. You can describe a process, "First you must find the car jack."

7. You can categorize your examples to help support a point.

8. You can define something, "Honesty is a virtue."

9. You can compare and contrast.

10. Go back and read the paragraphs in this chapter on argument, or statement and proof.

11. The tone of your essay reveals your attitude; the basic tone can be formal or informal.

12. You can begin your essay with a background statement, a question, a story, a fact, or a definition.

CHAPTER Six

The Systematic Approach to Essay Composition

There are two main keys to essay writing, as I have said from the beginning of this book. The first is discovering your point of view about the topic. You can do this by *Thinking Around the Box*™ using Contextual Thinking with diagramming and freewriting or one of the shortcut methods we discussed, Spider Diagrams and Lists. This chapter looks more closely at the second key, disclosing your point of view in your essay.

DISCLOSING YOUR POINT OF VIEW

Disclosure begins by divulging your main thesis. You reveal this in the first paragraph; preferably in the first sentence. You help set the tone by the way you introduce your thesis. Let's assume that the topic for consideration is the proverb "Honesty is always the best policy."

You can turn this into a **statement:** "Honesty is one of the fundamental virtues of society." Now you can go on to show this to be true or untrue.

You can turn this into a **question:** "Have you ever wondered if honesty is always the best policy?" You must, then, come down on one side or the other.

You could turn this into a **story:** "When I was young, an incident occurred that once and for all taught me that honesty is indeed the best policy."

You can also turn this into a straightforward **factual approach,** which suits some writers more than others: "The fact that only one tenth of 1 percent of Americans are behind bars means that honesty is the choice of the majority."

Lastly, you can turn this into a **definition,** which is a favorite device for many essay writers: "Honesty is a virtue and virtue is defined as having a quality of moral excellence. Society as a whole benefits in direct proportion to the number of citizens who practice moral excellence."

The thesis statement, no matter how it is introduced (statement, question, narrative, fact, or definition), must be specific and unambiguous. Taking both sides of an issue and arguing both is not to be recommended in a five-paragraph, 250- to 300-word essay. It is not only difficult, but it also reveals ambivalence on the part of the writer.

The tone, determined by the type of introduction and the specific content and language, should be appropriate to the topic. If the subject matter is capital punishment, a humorous question would probably not set the right tone.

The thesis statement is the appetizer. It must capture your reader's attention and set expectations. It brings the reader into your world. It tells them to listen and promises that the read will be worthwhile. It states both the issue and your position and contains the seeds of your argument.

Suppose that your essay topic is this: *Cities are just as good a place to live as the suburbs and small towns.*

First, of course, you use *Thinking Around the Box*™ on the subject matter raised by the topic and decide on a thesis or point of view. Then, you must convey your position in such a way as to leave the reader in no doubt as to how you feel. You must also clearly state the issue and your position in a way that will encourage the reader to carry on. Furthermore, the statement must contain the seeds of your argument.

For this topic, a background statement might look like this: "Large cities have become challenging places to live due to higher costs, traffic congestion, and increasing crime." With this, you have left no doubt as to the position (thesis) you have taken on the issue. Your reader can look forward to another three paragraphs addressing costs, traffic, and crime, in turn, to prove your point, and a final paragraph summing up what you have said.

Of course, you could also convey the exact same position, but set a different tone by beginning with a question. "Have you ever wondered what it would be like to live in a city? From the news reports that I see, I am sure that the costs, traffic, and higher crime rates would not make life any easier." Or, you could tell a story: "Until I was 12, I lived in Chicago. My parents decided to move to the suburbs, citing the expense, traffic, and crime of the city." **A caution:** the position taken here is an echo of the writer's parents, not necessarily the writer, unless she or he goes on in the rest of the essay to prove them right. Naturally, a statistical approach with plenty of facts may well be the one to take. Keep in mind that this will not do if you are in an exam room with no access to the facts about comparative costs, traffic, and crime.

A definition statement in this case probably would not work, since you would have to describe and define urban living. Such a definition is not all that likely to help you draw a reader in.

Clearly, the type of essay topic you get lends itself to a particular tone. In the case of the essay about city living, a formal, straightforward background statement works well, as does a less formal question or an informal story, either of which could develop a quite serious tone. Remember that, in addition to the tone you choose, there are techniques to be employed.

An **illustration** might be used. For example, "During the last year we lived in Chicago, my father's commute time to his office doubled due to road construction." You might include detailed, vivid **descriptions** of a scene where you witnessed two muggings on your block in two months; that would draw the reader in and lead them to your conclusion. **Comparisons** and

contrasts between living conditions in a large-city environment and a suburban or rural setting also would provide solid evidence. Remember that you are arguing a position. Check your logic.

Let's take the background statement approach to the essay question.

essay

Cities are just as good a place to live as the suburbs and small towns.

Large cities have become challenging places to live due to higher costs, traffic congestion, and increasing crime. (*This is a good thesis statement; it states your opinion clearly and contains the seeds of the next three paragraphs—i.e., costs, traffic, and crime.*) I have never lived in a large city, and my knowledge of them is limited to newspaper and TV reports and a short trip to New York City last year with my school band. (*This body sentence in the first paragraph is a disclaimer, but it shows that you are paying attention.*) My memories from that visit were of meals that cost twice as much as in my hometown, but which were not twice as good, and crowds of people and nonstop vehicle traffic. My feeling that the city is more dangerous than my hometown comes from the news reports. I did not see any crimes during my visit. (*These body sentences lend support to why you feel the way you do about cities.*)

Prices seemed to be on everyone's mind. (*Topic sentence for the second paragraph takes on a narrative technique*) The movies as well as the meals were almost double the prices I am used to. I discovered from a young student who was our waitress that she was from a town near where I live. She told me that her income was nowhere near twice what it was in her hometown. She had to share a small apartment with three other students. (*These four body sentences support the topic sentence—cost—and the thesis.*)

Getting around the city with a bulky case containing my French horn was a problem. (*Topic sentence*) One evening, two of my friends decided to walk to the hall where we were to perform. Three of us decided to take a taxi. My mother had insisted that we do this. The traffic at each intersection became worse and worse. In the end, we arrived at the hall 10 minutes late. My friends, who had walked, got there 10 minutes ahead of us, and we were $15 poorer. (*These body sentences support the paragraph topic—traffic—and the overall thesis.*)

Like prices and traffic, crime also seemed to be on everyone's mind. (*Topic sentence*) After our concert, we went for a hamburger. The waiter told us that the restaurant had been robbed twice in the year he had worked there. Like most Americans, I have seen many reports of big-city crime, and I have watched some of the TV crime shows that all seem to take place in large cites. It does not paint a pretty picture. (*These body sentences support the topic sentence—crime—and thesis.*)

My hometown is small; too small for a major league sports franchise. New York is home to several. The price people literally pay to live there, however, plus the congestion they suffer and the fear they feel means I have no desire to move from my small town. (*Conclusion sentences*)

TRANSITIONAL WORDS AND PHRASES

This essay is technically quite correct. It obeys the rules for writing a competent 1-3-1, 250- to 350-word essay. However, it reads in a fairly stilted, formal, or awkward manner. This can be corrected somewhat by the introduction of transitional words and phrases, which can be categorized by what they have to do with:

- **Time:** *after, at last, before, during, eventually, finally, later, meanwhile, soon, while, when*
- **Importance:** *above all, especially, in fact, in particular, more important, most important, worst of all*
- **Example:** *for example, for instance, one reason*
- **Additions:** *and, additionally, also, another, as well as, furthermore, in addition to, moreover, another thing to consider*
- **Condition:** *but, although, however, in contrast, instead, nevertheless, on the other hand, still, yet*
- **Replacements for the word "so":** *as a result, in summary, because, finally, therefore*

Try rereading the above essay and fitting in a few of the transitional words and phrases to see if you can make the essay a better read. I can see, for example, where the word "although" could be added. I can also see where the phrase "most important" would be helpful. You can find other useful additions, I'm sure.

Adding a transitional word or phrase frequently suggests a slight adjustment to the sentence structure. The last sentence could, for instance, read like this: "In summary, the price people pay, quite literally, to live there, as well as the erosion of their quality of life because of congestion and fear means I have no desire to leave my hometown."

THE BULL'S-EYE PARAGRAPH

Some of the more adventurous among my readers might want to experiment by writing an essay with what I call a "bull's-eye" paragraph. This is a technique whereby you write the last paragraph first and make the preceding paragraphs lead up to it, or aim for it. (You should *only* do this if, during your freewriting of ideas, you come up with an obvious and eye-popping concluding paragraph that neatly summarizes and ties all the other ideas together. This will eventually happen if you practice, practice, practice *Thinking Around the Box*^{TM}.)

For instance, suppose that you are given the task of writing an essay on pollution. In the process of thinking about the subject in context, you jot down some ideas. For example, "pollution is a man-made problem," or, "if this activity is allowed to continue, it may result in the sacrifice of innocent lives in the pursuit of profit," or, "man is the cause and man must be the cure." Perhaps one of the ideas that might come to mind is the fact that coal miners in the nineteenth century used to carry canaries into the mines. If toxic gases were present, the birds would die. This would warn the miners not to proceed until the danger was averted.

Perhaps you agree that this fact could be written into the last paragraph first, then used as a target, or bull's-eye, that the four preceding paragraphs could aim for. Lots of crime or detective writers have written the last scene first, then gone back to write the beginning. A bull's-eye, or final, essay paragraph, in the case of the pollution essay, might look like this:

In the early days of the Industrial Revolution, coal miners took canaries down into the mines with them to warn of poisonous gases. The lesson from these workers and their poor canaries was, of course, simple; to ignore early warning signs of an unhealthy environment was to invite annihilation. Taking the place of those unfortunate canaries, in the twenty-first century, are changing weather patterns, holes in the ozone, and global warming. We ignore them at our peril, or, rather, at our grandchildren's peril.

If you were now to take all of the other thoughts, ideas, and inklings that you had written when thinking about the issue of pollution, do you think you could write the first four paragraphs aiming at that conclusion? I bet you could. Perhaps the opening paragraph would be something like this:

> The issue of pollution is important to me because I am young and also live in an ecologically fragile area of the USA. Pollution takes many forms. I see them all taking their toll. Pleasure seekers are injuring our wildlife by putting their own needs for water above the needs of our planet. Smokestacks are wreaking havoc with our air. Noise is as much a kind of pollution as any highway billboard. I would like to hand a better, cleaner environment to my children than my parents handed to me.

Now you write the middle three paragraphs. The thesis is there—you don't have to agree or disagree with it—and the seeds of the next paragraphs are also there, as is the concluding paragraph. It could almost write itself. (It helps hone your skills to write essays with a thesis you do not agree with, just as it helps debate teams to debate positions they don't avow. It's great practice!)

KNOWING YOUR AUDIENCE

No matter who your readers are, speak plainly. Leave no room for interpretation. Be specific. Use punctuation to make sure that you say what you mean.

Look at the following cartoon for a minute. Then ask yourself "Is this a duck gazing off to the left, or is this a rabbit looking to the right?

The answer of course becomes clear after a minute: it's both, in which case, it's neither. It's ambiguous and, therefore, unclear. Never, ever leave your readers in a state of ambiguity.

"I haven't seen nothing," is a common enough expression, and completely imprecise. "Haven't" is a negative. "Nothing" is a negative, and two negatives cancel one another out to make a positive. So, when the speaker said "I haven't seen nothing," he or she probably meant that they had not seen anything. Their chosen method of expressing this thought, however, expresses the exact opposite. "I have not seen nothing" means "I have seen something." Preciseness, like cleanliness, is next to godliness.

Here is a brief movie review I read recently in my local newspaper:

Jeff Bridges and Kim Basinger star as a couple coping with the deaths of their children in different ways.

The writer of this piece violated the first rule of writing: write so that people will understand what you mean. It is unclear, and that is the problem. Did the children die in different ways, or is the couple coping in different ways?

The writer should have written her review as either:

> Jeff Bridges and Kim Basinger star as a couple coping, in different ways, with the deaths of their children.

or

> Jeff Bridges and Kim Basinger star as a couple coping with the different manners in which their children met their ends.

Well-intended sentences can be rendered absurd by the insertion or deletion of punctuation. The title of a recent best-selling book was suggested to the author Lynne Truss, when she saw this partial description of the giant panda: "The giant panda eats, shoots and leaves." The insertion of a single errant comma after the word "eats" changes the sentence from an intended description of the animal's typical diet to a cartoon image in the mind of the reader of a panda bear having a meal, shooting a pistol, and then departing.

It really comes down to paying attention to what you write and how you write it. In a way, it's all about respect: respect for your subject, your audience, and—above all—yourself.

In writing an essay, you are talking to an audience that cannot talk back. Unlike a face-to-face conversation, you cannot see their faces to gauge their reaction. You cannot ask for questions, and then use those questions as cues and clues. If the people reading your work make a face, shrug, sigh, cry, smile, or otherwise respond, it is hidden from you. These same readers are separated from you by distance and time. It may be weeks before they sit down in Arizona, Iowa, or New Jersey to read what you wrote in Texas, New York, or California. You can only guess that they understand **exactly** what you meant. (By the way, the best way of improving the odds of being understood is to follow the principles laid out in this book.)

When it comes to knowing *your* audience, you have some distinct advantages. You can, with a degree of certainty, make some assumptions about readers of essays written by high school students. To begin with, it is their profession to do so. They do this for a living. This means the readers of your essays are expert at what they do. They read a lot of essays. They are also likely to be well versed in the English language.

So, first, write with a skeptical reader in mind. A skeptic is one who doubts and questions everything—a disbeliever who has to be convinced. If your logic is flawed, if evidence is irrelevant, then the skeptic will never be convinced. By consciously writing for the reader with a skeptical mind, you make sure that you have set the bar at the right height.

Take some time to think about your audience. The college admissions director and the person marking your SAT or ACT Assessment essay see a lot of essays. What they are looking for is your skill in taking on the topic, your ability to organize your thoughts, your ability to develop your ideas into a thoughtful point of view through critical thinking, and your skill at conveying all of this in a clear, concise manner using Standard Written English. "Plain," "simple," "sincere," and "orderly" should be prominent among the adjectives that your readers use to express their opinion about your work.

EDITING YOUR ESSAY

If you are to write the best possible essay, you must leave time for polishing. Let's say you have 25 minutes to write your essay. Five minutes should go into designing your essay; this is the discovery part. Allow 15 minutes for disclosure, or writing the essay, and 5 minutes for editing your work. **You must practice**. In Chapter 12, there is a list of 100 essay topics for you to work on.

Editing Checklist

❑ Does your first paragraph contain a thesis sentence that expresses the controlling idea and conveys your point of view?

❑ Does your topic or thesis sentence contain some of the elements (seeds) that you will expand on later?

❑ Does each sentence you have written express a complete thought using a subject and a verb?

❑ Do all the body or support sentences in your first paragraph relate to, *and support,* the thought expressed in your first sentence?

❑ Do all of the paragraphs begin with a sentence that expresses a thought that is part of the overall argument?

❑ Are all the support sentences relevant to the main idea of the paragraph in which they appear?

❑ Do you tie all the pieces together in your last paragraph to bring the reader to a conclusion?

❑ Are all your paragraphs indented?

❑ Do you use transitional words and phrases to tie the paragraphs together?

❑ Is the essay written in the accepted style of Standard Written English?

❑ If you were of a different opinion, what openings for an attack do you see in your argument?

Now read your essay out loud. You will be surprised at how good an editing trick this is. Your reader "hears" your work this way.

Finally, what does the essay say about you? Remember that your readers also judge. They are not so much interested in your actual views on honesty, television, or school uniforms as in your *voice.* Is it an authentic voice, one with a clear idea of what to communicate and a clear way of expressing your point of view? Will they get the idea that you are a person with integrity, a sense of identity, and style? Will they hear a confident, passionate voice or a hesitant one? Have you conveyed thoughtfulness and maturity, or not? These are the qualities any examiner will respond to, no matter whether they are a teacher, a college admissions officer, or a potential employer. If the reader cannot see you in person, the essay becomes your only opportunity to show how special you are. Even an SAT/ACT Assessment reader is likely to be receptive to an authentic voice.

I wrote the following 1-3-1, 321-word essay in answer to the question: *Who was your favorite teacher*? Look it over to see if you can "check off" all of the questions listed on the previous two pages. Find the two (or more) mistakes.

essay

Who was your favorite teacher?

My eighth-grade teacher, Mr. Jones, was my favorite because he brought a sense of fun to his classroom to improve the learning atmosphere and discipline and to show us the relevance of social studies. He once had us all dress as revolutionary heroes of the War of Independence. My sister helped me dress up as Ben Franklin. We all soon learned the value of a democracy. Mr. Jones made us argue for independence as if we were the Founding Fathers. Mr. Jones was Welsh and I like the Welsh people.

Of course, it is difficult to learn if the classroom is out of control. Mr. Jones never let this happen. Now, four years later, I realize that it was his sense of humor that helped him control the students. His personality made it difficult for anyone not to like him. If the atmosphere in the classroom became tense, he always had a joke ready to defuse the situation.

Even if Mr. Jones needed to discipline a student, he always did it without any nastiness. I remember one very rude boy who never smiled. Mr. Jones patiently involved him in our play-acting, and by the end of the school year, the boy was quite friendly.

Social Studies in seventh grade were our least favorite subject. None of us could see the point of learning about history and geography. It was boring and dull to have to learn about India and China and politics. Mr. Jones dressed one day as a poor Chinese peasant. He taught us that people in other countries are not as fortunate as we are.

For me personally, learning was made fun. Mr. Jones did this so well that I have decided to become a teacher myself. There are too many serious lessons that have to be passed on from one generation to another. We shouldn't leave it all to the boring and dull teachers. Learning can be fun.

Here are some mistakes within the essay:

- Not many transitional words and phrases are used, leading to a choppy tone.
- The fact that Mr. Jones was Welsh is interesting, but not relevant to the argument.
- "For me personally," is an example of redundancy. Either "for me" or "personally" would be fine, but do not use both.
- "Learning was made fun" is the passive voice. You get top marks if you spotted this one.
- Here's another tricky one: Social Studies is a single subject, so it takes a singular verb: "*Social Studies . . . was* our least favorite *subject*." (Social Studies relates directly to the singular word "subject" at the end of the sentence.)

In Short

1. Having discovered your point of view by *Thinking Around the Box*™, make sure your thesis is specific and unambiguous.

2. Choose the type of introduction, content, and language that will set an appropriate tone for your essay.

3. When writing, use transitional words and phrases to link paragraphs seamlessly together.

4. Use the "Bull's-Eye" method *only* if you are confident. That confidence is a result of *practice*.

5. Think about your audience—assume they are skeptical.

6. Edit your essay.

CHAPTER SEVEN

The Rules of Style

The soul of your essay is its message. It is the content and substance of what you write about. Just as a painter's self and soul escape onto the canvas by way of the brush, conveying a message in colors, perspective, and brushstrokes, the writing style is the *sound* words make on paper. That sound can convey the message with harmony or cover it over with static. This is why it is so important that you read your work out loud as you write.

Your readers will never get to the soul of your essay if your style gets in the way. If, however, the style is clear, accurate, and concise, then the message of your essay will be delivered.

Here are some hints, suggestions, and outright rules that must not be broken. Take the time to learn them all. Breaking these rules takes the reader away from your message as quickly and completely as the singer singing out of tune. I have selected some examples of the rules of style. There are many others and many books devoted to them. Take the time to learn them.

GRAMMAR

Grammar covers a lot of ground. To keep you from drifting off into a daydream as you review the selected examples, I have broken them up into four categories. The categories are: general items and advice, overused and incorrectly used terms, incorrect and superfluous terms and constructions, and "pet peeves" that I find really annoying.

General Items and Advice

- Avoid clutter. "He climbed the misty mountain," is just fine. "He groped his way through the opaque mist as he clambered to the summit of the shrouded pinnacle" is not fine in an essay. In a novel, this would be acceptable language.

- Do not use qualifiers. "I am *pretty* sure," or "it is *rather* hot," or "he can do a *little* better."

- Never use the word "like" incorrectly. "He could run like a deer" is correct. "He could like run, you know" might be how your friends speak—count the number of times your friends use the word "like" in a sentence—but it is incorrect English.

- There is a big difference between writing and conversation. "Remember, dude, you know, like you and me and the team, like we were hanging at the beach and these old folks looked at us like we were from Mars." Do *not* adopt the tone, grammar, and syntax of conversational slang—no exceptions.

- Do not use "netspeak," instant messaging, or blog shorthand. Type "u" for *you* and "u" will fail.

- We are all exposed to advertising jargon. It might be acceptable for advertisers to refer to something as having been "obsoleted," but this is not even a word that Microsoft's spell checker recognizes. A car or a dress or a pair of sneakers cannot be "cool;" a glass of iced tea can. Be careful that you do not appear uneducated or ignorant.

- Simplify in order to clarify. Which of the following sentences simplifies and clarifies?

Wheat is used for feeding purposes.

or

Wheat is used for food.

If you guessed the second one, you are right. The first sentence exemplifies a mistake called "overwriting." Look at any government pamphlet to find many other examples.

- Again with an eye to brevity, do not write "He is a man who is very ambitious." The correct and shorter sentence should read "He is a very ambitious man." Or, since the word "he" implies "man," you could simply write "He is very ambitious."

- Another helpful hint, when clarifying or abbreviating, is never to use the phrase "in terms of." "The job was unsatisfactory in terms of salary" should be written "The salary made the job unsatisfactory." Use plain English.

- The use of verbs can make or break an essay. Their normal function is to express action or existence. "He moved the crowd with his speech." This verb, "moved," expresses action. "He is his own man." This verb, "is," expresses existence. Verbs, however, can be suggestive, as in "Rain symbolizes growth." Verbs can reinforce an idea: "The light emphasizes the beauty of the painting." Verbs can hint: "Her demeanor implied a wealthy upbringing." Verbs can be descriptive and visual, as in "He focuses only on success."

- If the subject is plural, then the verb must be plural. "The race cars (plural) are (plural) speeding." Not "the race cars is speeding." The reverse is also true. What's wrong with this sentence? "The principal's sense of humor are an asset."

- If you have used the words "each," "each one," "everybody," or "everyone," do not use the word "they" in the next part of the sentence. "Everyone knows they are human" is wrong. "Everyone knows he or she is human" is correct. Of course, this leads us to gender. To avoid overusing "he or she," one could write "We all know we are human."

- It may sound politically correct, but "their" and "theirs" are plural possessive words and are not to used with singular pronouns "he" or "she," which take the singular possessives "his" and "hers."

- The noun "media" is plural. So, in a sentence, make sure that the verb agrees with the noun: "The media were well represented at the convention" is correct.

- The infamous "split infinitive" occurs when a word is inserted in between the word "to" and the verb it refers to. It's often easy to correct this problem. For example, "I sometimes like to slowly eat my favorite ice cream, enjoying the flavor and the texture," can become "I sometimes like to eat my favorite ice cream slowly, enjoying the flavor and the texture." The changed version has the same meaning and sounds fine. In some cases, however, a "corrected" version just wouldn't work, and great writers know this. So Captain Kirk, along with all his other achievements, splits the infinitive when he says, "To boldly go where no man has gone before." That sentence would not have the same ring to it without the split infinitive, would it?

- Prepositions are words that describe the position that something or someone has in relation to something else. The following are examples of prepositions: *about, around, at, between, by, down, for, from, in, of, out, over, to, under,* and *with.* "The man is in the car." In this sentence, the word "in" describes the relationship of the man to the car. In general, the rule is never to end a sentence with a preposition. This is a rule that most of the great writers have flouted. "I will not leave thee, until I have done that which I have spoken to thee *of.*" That's from the Bible. "Out of Paris came a treaty that few had dared hope *for.*" That was the report of a journalist in London, in 1919, after the treaty ending the First World War. Shakespeare regularly ended sentences with prepositions. You probably should not.

- Synonyms are words that mean the same thing or words that come close to meaning the same thing. If you find yourself writing a sentence that requires that you use the word "friend" more than once, the temptation is to use a synonym in the second or third instance. If, in the next sentence, you find yourself having to use the word "friend" once more, it is time to pause. The reason is that synonyms are rarely exact duplicates. "Colleague," "comrade," "companion," "associate," and "acquaintance" all have slightly different connotations. Can an associate be a friend? Possibly, but not necessarily. Can an acquaintance also be a friend? No. In most cases, repeating the word is a necessity. It might not look elegant, but it will leave the reader in no doubt, and that is the main goal of essay writing.

- "That" or "which?" The word "that" defines or restricts an object: "The car that is in the garage has broken down." This sentence suggests there are other cars—perhaps in the driveway or on the street. The car is defined, or identified, as the one in the garage. The word "which" is not restrictive; it is preceded by a comma and adds a fact. "The car, which is in the garage, has broken down." This sentence suggests there is only one car. Its location is merely additional information.

- The word "this" can cause confusion because it is not always clear what "this" refers to. The classic example used by all grammarians is as follows:

> Visiting dignitaries watched yesterday as the ground was broken for the new physics laboratory with the new safety wall. This is the first evidence of the university's plans for modernization.

The word "this" at the beginning of the second sentence does not make it clear enough to what it is referring. Is it the wall or the lab? Replace "this is" by the phrase "The ceremony provided," and precision is achieved.

Overused and Incorrectly Used Terms

- The word "leave" is often used incorrectly. "Leave go of that rope" is not correct. "Let go of that rope" is correct.
- "Like" is frequently and incorrectly used in place of "as." Do not write "We celebrated the holiday like in the old days." Correct your sentence to read "We celebrated the holidays as in the old days."
- "Literally" is one of the most misused and overused words. The word means that something is strictly true. "The principal was literally breathing fire" should not be written down unless she was "literally" giving a demonstration of fire-breathing by inhaling, tasting gasoline, and setting fire to it as she exhaled the fumes. If you say "the man was

literally dead from fatigue," you have just informed your reader of a fact. If you meant to simply exaggerate, then you have not done so. But, you have confused your reader. Was the man dead or very tired?

- "Incredible" is another overworked word. Listen to any unimaginative reporter on TV and count the number of times he or she uses the word. It means "hard to believe" or "implausible," even if they interchange it with its synonym, "unbelievable."

- The word "unique" means one of a kind. To say "very unique" is like saying "very one of a kind."

- Most of the time the word "personally" is redundant. "Personally, I liked the book." Brevity is the essence of clarity. "I liked the book" will suffice; the word "I" establishes quite clearly who is speaking. I recently overheard this example of a triple redundancy. "In my opinion, I personally think smoking should be banned." This was extremely irritating to hear; to see it written invites low marks.

- "Disinterested" or "uninterested?" To be disinterested is to be impartial or unbiased, ready to hear both sides of the argument. In court it is desirable to have jurors who are disinterested. To be uninterested is to be without interest.

- "Kind of" and "sort of" may only be used in the correct way. "A hawk is a kind of bird." What does "I am sort of tired" mean? Are you tired or aren't you?

- "Imply" and "infer" have very different meanings and are not interchangeable. To imply is to suggest something. To infer is to deduce or conclude something to be correct. "Farming implies rising early." Contrast that with "Since she is a farmer, we can infer that she rises early."

- "Nor" is another word that gives people fits. "She cannot eat nor sleep" is incorrect. "She cannot eat or sleep" is correct, as is "She can neither eat nor sleep." Use "nor" only in combination with "neither."

- "Farther" or "further," which one to use? "Farther" refers only to distance. "He drove a little farther down the road." "Further" may refer to distance, time, or quantity. "He pursued his dreams further." So, if either time or quantity is involved, be sure to use "further."

Incorrect and Superfluous Terms and Constructions

- After the phrase "regarded as," you do not need the word "being." "He is regarded as being the best football player in school" is best written as "He is regarded as the best football player in school."
- "In regards to" and "with regards to" are both incorrect. "In regard to" and "with regard to" are correct; "regarding" is even better.
- Use "in less than" rather than "inside of." "In less than 5 minutes, I will be home" is fine.
- "Any body" versus "anybody." The first means any physical body or corpse, the second any person. The same holds true for "some body" and "somebody," "no body" and "nobody," and "every body" and "everybody."
- "Care less" and "careless." To care less about someone or something is to dismiss its importance. "Careless" is a synonym for negligent.
- The correct use of the word "try" is followed by the word "to," not the word "and." "Try to fix" is correct; "try and fix" is not.
- Do not "consider" something "as." The sentence "I consider him as incompetent" is better written as "I consider him incompetent."
- After the words "doubt" or "help," it is not correct to insert "but." It is incorrect to write "I have no doubt *but* that he is the best football player in school" or "I could not help *but* notice her freckles."
- The word "case" or "cases" is often superfluous, as in the sentence "In many cases the rooms were unheated." It would be better to write "Many of the rooms were unheated."
- The suffix "-wise." The random addition of the word "wise" as a suffix, done in particular by TV sports commentators and weather persons, is both an abomination and lazy. "Weather-wise we are in for some showers." Aaargh! "Yardage-wise, this has not been a good quarter for the home team." Aaargh again! "Fashion-wise," "performance-wise," "runproduction-wise," "acceptance-wise"—I have heard all of them and hear the collapse of our civilization in their echoes. If, heaven forbid, you were to write "School-wise, I am quite pleased with my

progress," you would assure your reader to the contrary. Almost any noun in the English language could have this suffix appended, but, with the exception of the noun "clock," don't do it.

Pet Peeves

- "And/or," we have all seen this term. The simple rule for you is to avoid its use at all costs.
- How about the word "anticipate." Use this word only in the context of an important event. To anticipate the birth of a child or the signing of a peace treaty adequately describes what is involved. To anticipate the arrival of the school bus sounds pretentious to me. The arrival of a bus is a more mundane or routine event, and it probably deserves a word such as "expect."
- Dynamite is an explosive chemical invented by Alfred Nobel. It is not properly considered an adjective, as in "She is a dynamite ball player."
- "Etc." Do not use this term. It is imprecise.
- "Fortuitous" refers to things happening by chance. I find using it to mean "lucky" or "fortunate" irritating and off the mark.
- "Get" and "got" and "gotten." Sometimes, I hear people use "have got" when "have" would be sufficient. "I have not got any money" is an unfortunate use of English to describe an unfortunate state of economic well-being. "I have no money" states the position correctly. "Gotten" is a word that is commonly used in speech. Do not use it in writing.
- "Gratuitous" does not mean "generous." It means "unnecessary" or "superfluous," as in "The film contained too much gratuitous violence."
- To my way of thinking, "insightful" describes the kind of theories that Einstein or Newton came up with. Try using "perceptive" in all other cases.
- "Irregardless" is not generally accepted as a word. "Regardless" clearly is.
- "Nice" is one the most imprecise words in the English language. It has no less than nine definitions in my dictionary. Avoid its use. To

describe Emily Dickinson's poetry or Mozart's music as nice, as I once did, is almost an insult. My teacher told me that I had just used the word "nice" to describe "The finger of God (Mozart) writing on the surface of the earth." I have never used the word "nice" since. Neither should you. Find another adjective at all costs.

- "-oriented." A recent import to the English language from business schools, hyphenating a word with "oriented" is an incorrect use of English. I recently heard a representative of a major university describe her institution as "academically-oriented." Is there any other kind of university, I wondered?

- "Relate" is a word that has crept into our language. "He and I relate to one another." The use of this word is likely to irritate a literate examiner; and it is safe to assume that they all are—literate, that is.

- Never use the word "utilize." The correct word is "use." Telling a reader that you utilized all the brainpower you could, assures them that the opposite is probably true.

I have picked out the above as just a few examples of the rules and suggestions for the correct usage of English. You must learn them in order to write English, just as you must learn your multiplication tables in order to calculate.

I suggest strongly that you do further reading in the various books written by the authorities on the subject, such as Strunk and White's *The Elements of Style* and *Style* by Joseph M. Williams. There are many others.

I cannot emphasize enough that your voice must be in tune, and that means the grammar and syntax must be accurate. Otherwise, you will redirect the reader away from your message. You do not want to do that in high school; you really do not want to do that in college; and you really, really do not want to do that in your career after college.

TROPES

"What?" you ask. Don't worry, this is just the generic word for all figures of speech. Now *you* can impress someone with your knowledge of English.

When we speak, or write, we do so in one of two ways. We either convey our message literally, or we convey our message metaphorically. We accomplish metaphorical communication all the time by using figurative speech, such as metaphors and similes. We also use other tropes such as analogies, hyperbole, understatement, and rhetorical questions.

When someone says "Bill is struggling with his studies," it is a literal statement of fact. When someone says "At school, Bill is like a fish struggling to swim upstream," it conveys the same meaning as a figure of speech, in this case a simile. In your writing, use figures of speech very sparingly.

- **Metaphors** are among our language's most persuasive devices. They imply a comparison between two unrelated things, and the imagery they conjure up adds an appeal to the reader's senses. The poet Robert Frost spoke of freedom as a horse that is easy in its harness. Life is often referred to as a stream. The later years of life are often called the evening or the twilight or the autumnal years. You will notice that the comparison is implied, there is no "like" or "as." Avoid mixing metaphors: "Life is a stream that flies by all too quickly." Streams don't fly and the reader, especially the expert reader, will not be impressed.

- **Similes** are where the words "like" or "as" come into play. A simile is a direct comparison. For example, "The golf ball landed softly on the green, like a butterfly with sore feet." The idea is to conjure up an image that conveys the message.

- **Analogies** are simply comparisons of two dissimilar things for special effect. It implies that if they are similar in one way, they may be similar in other ways: "If automobiles had developed like computers, they would now cost $500, exceed the speed of sound, and run forever on a battery." Or, "The mighty Mississippi is to the Midwest what an artery is to the body; each carries life to all the parts it serves."

- **Hyperbole** is the deliberate use of overstatement for literary effect: "She's worth a gazillion dollars." It is probably not a good idea to use hyperbole in essays. You should, however, know what it is.

- **Understatement.** Writing that "Napoleon knew how to get on in the world" certainly understates the little dictator's achievements. The discoverers of DNA, Watson and Crick, came as close as anyone to discovering the meaning of life. Yet, in commenting on their achievement, the two scientists wrote, "It has not escaped our notice that our discovery suggests a possible copying mechanism for genetic material." This is the academic understatement of the twentieth century, or perhaps any century. Genius is modest, indeed.

- **Rhetorical Questions** are questions that really do not require answers. Instead, they help to support or contradict a position, as in this example: "Have you ever wondered how Congress makes decisions?" The writer now might go on to satirize the decision-making of our House of Representatives or to simply explain how decisions are made. Either way, a rhetorical question is a trope worth using.

- **Irony and Sarcasm.** Irony is the use of a word such as "honorable" in a context where the reader is expected to get the exact opposite impression. In Shakespeare's play *Julius Caesar*, Mark Antony repeatedly criticizes Brutus, who has just killed Caesar, by repeating Brutus's claim that he is honorable again and again: "But Brutus is an honorable man." Sarcasm is the act of mocking people or being contemptuous of them or their achievements, behavior, attire, or demeanor: "I wonder which yard sale that outfit came from." I would not recommend attempting either of these literary devices.

PUNCTUATION

The first writers did not use punctuation; they just kept on adding words. The only punctuation used was to separate words with white spaces, assuming they were using paper and not clay. About 2,300 years ago, Aristophanes of Byzantium, a librarian at the great Library of Alexandria in Egypt, made a stab at punctuation. His reasons for doing this have not been lost to us; he wanted to show the actors, who read from manuscripts, where to take a breath. He invented the comma, which meant to *cut off*. People who write about this kind of thing have been quarreling about its usage ever since.

Nowadays, in fact, people argue incessantly about punctuation in general. They write books on the subject or letters to the editor. The little dots and dashes that make up punctuation marks are supposed to make reading easier by giving the reader either time to breathe or hints as to meaning. They accomplish this *only* when the author makes correct decisions about their usage.

When we talk, we use punctuation of a different sort. We raise and lower our voices, we take a breath, or we emphasize certain words or phrases. Punctuation is the equivalent of these vocal clues. Periods are the equivalent of normal pauses. Semicolons and colons indicate somewhat shorter pauses. The beginning of a new paragraph indicates a much longer pause.

Let's look at the most common forms of punctuation and the rules for their use.

- **The apostrophe (').** The rules for the use of an apostrophe vary a little. An apostrophe (') shows either possession or the omission of a letter or sound. Apostrophes do this by modifying the word. For example, when showing possession, such as in the statement "John F. Kennedy's presidency," the apostrophe is inserted after the last letter of the word in question and the letter "s" is added. It is simply another way of saying "The presidency of John F. Kennedy." Note that if the word ends in an "s," then another *s* is added—"James's bicycle." Possessive pronouns such as *hers, his, its, ours, theirs,* and *yours* do not use apostrophes. Contractions are formed by the omission of a letter or sound, and the omission is symbolized by the apostrophe. Contractions include "don't" for "do not," "won't" for "will not," "it's" for "it is," and "can't" for "cannot."

> To check whether the word "its" takes an apostrophe or not, ask yourself whether you would use "it is" for "its." The sentence "It's my dog's bowl" means "It is my dog's bowl." But in the sentence "My dog eats from its bowl," you cannot substitute the words "it is," because writing "My dog eats from it is bowl" makes no sense.

- **The colon (:).** The purpose of the colon is to introduce something or someone. "The best baseball players in history have the following names: Babe Ruth, Lou Gehrig, Ted Williams, and Hank Aaron."
- **The semicolon (;).** The semicolon connects two thoughts that are related but independent: "The films of George Lucas are entertaining; they are filled with novel ideas." Or, "Speech is silver; silence is golden."
- **The comma (,).** Think of the comma as a short breath that you might take when speaking; it allows the sentence to take a break. A comma follows an introductory phrase: "On the fourth of July, Independence Day is observed." Or, "Inspired by the sunset, the artist painted her best work." Or, "If this is the best you can do, you probably should find another line of work." Commas appear before and after an aside, or parenthetical phrase: "Abraham Lincoln, the sixteenth president of the United States, was born in 1861 in Illinois." Commas appear between items in a list, including the next-to-last item: "The family picked up and moved lock, stock, and barrel." Commas also appear between city and state and day and year: "Chicago, Illinois" and "July 4, 2004."
- **The exclamation mark (!).** The exclamation mark is used to demonstrate strong feeling. "He is guilty as sin!" One exclamation mark is enough; two or more reveal ignorance of correct punctuation!

- **The question mark (?).** The question mark ends a sentence that asks for information. "What is the meaning of life?"
- **The period (.).** The period ends a sentence where an exclamation mark or question mark is not appropriate. In England, this is known as a *full stop*, which more exactly describes its function.
- **Quotation marks (" ").** Quotation marks are used around the titles of articles, songs, photographs, most poems, TV episodes, and most unpublished works. If you are referring to a book, a play, a very long poem, or the name of a ship within a sentence, *italics*, not quotation marks are correct: "Shakespeare's *King Lear* is among his most famous tragedies." Or, "Samuel Taylor Coleridge's *The Rime of the Ancient Mariner* was first published in 1798." If you are quoting someone or quoting from a published work, then quotation marks are used: Franklin D. Roosevelt said "The only thing we have to fear is fear itself." Or, The local newspaper described the fire as "one of the most devastating in the town's history." If you are quoting within a quote, use single quotation marks: The speaker said "The most important goal set by a president in the past 50 years was when John F. Kennedy said 'We will send a man to the moon in my lifetime.'"
- **The dash (—).** The dash separates two clauses (thoughts) more abruptly than a comma, colon, or semicolon. It is used for effect. The following sentence indicates, by use of a dash, an opinion or comment by the author about the subject. "His first thought upon getting out of bed—if he was thinking at all—was to get back into bed." Note that there is no space before or after a dash.

As we have seen, an error in punctuation can render a sentence either meaningless or meaning something the writer did not intend—it is debatable which one is worse. A writer who is in high school, however, can take comfort from an American editor called George Prentice who, in 1860, said "Many writers profess great exactness in punctuation, who never yet made a point."

In other words, it is important to say what you mean through the accurate use of sentence construction and punctuation. It is even more important to mean what you say.

APPLYING THE RULES OF STYLE

Grammar

1. If you want to be specific about which car you are referring to, which of the following two sentences would be correct?
   (a) The car that needs oil is in the garage.
   (b) The car, which needs oil, is in the garage.

2. Which of the following two statements contains a grammatical error, and what is the error?
   (a) He failed to diligently study his homework assignment.
   (b) He failed to research diligently his homework assignment.

3. What is wrong with this sentence?

   Are there a minimum age for voting in the United States?

4. What is wrong with the following sentences?
   (a) The teacher was rather clear about her subject matter.
   (b) The teacher was very clear about her subject matter.
   (c) The teacher was pretty clear about her subject matter.

5. Why is one of these two sentences clearer than the other one?
   (a) "Now, my boy, we shall see," he said, "how well you have learned your lesson."
   (b) "Now, my boy," he said, "we shall see how well you have learned your lesson."

6. What is wrong with the following sentence?

   The *de facto* standards for driving a taxi are laid out in the test manual.

7. What is wrong with this sentence?

   Every body who has tackled this theory was trained as an astronomer.

8. What is wrong with this sentence?

   If I was the president, all Americans would have health insurance now.

9. The following two sentences are guilty of the same error—what is it?
    (a) The company thrives because it is constantly introducing new innovations to the market.
    (b) I will meet you at 8 a.m. tomorrow morning.

Tropes

1. What is wrong with the following sentence?

The golf ball landed softly as a butterfly on the putting green, after a swing that was as smooth as glass and as accurate as a laser.

2. What is wrong with this sentence?

The issues surrounding the pharmaceutical industry are clouded in a sea of regulations, which are as dense as a thicket.

3. Which is the best of the following figures of speech, and why?
    (a) All the world's a stage.
    (b) All the world is like a stage.
    (c) All the world is as a stage.

4. What is wrong with this sentence?

A gardener is like a surgeon—always pruning, tying, cutting, and trimming.

5. What is wrong with the following sentence?

The man knew he had to eat soon and foraged with the same desperation as a grizzly bear catching salmon.

Punctuation

1. Which is the correct way to express the possessive case (form) for the following statement?

The family of Prince Charles
    (a) Prince Charles family

(b) Prince Charles' family

(c) Prince Charles's family

2. Which is the correctly punctuated sentence?

(a) The best way to see Vermont unless you are in a hurry is on foot.

(b) The best way to see Vermont, unless you are in a hurry, is on foot.

(c) The best way to see Vermont, unless you are in a hurry is on foot.

3. This sentence does not make much sense unless you insert a comma in just the right place. Can you put the comma in the right place?

Peter walked on his head a little higher than usual.

4. See how you can use punctuation to reverse the meaning of this sentence.

The accused said the judge is mad.

5. Which of the following has the correct punctuation?

(a) Bill has four brothers, Frank, Jack, Harry, and Andrew.

(b) Bill has four bothers; Frank, Jack, Harry, and Andrew.

(c) Bill has four brothers: Frank, Jack, Harry, and Andrew.

ANSWERS

Grammar

1. Sentence (a) is correct because the word "that" defines, or identifies, something. In sentence (b), apparently there is only one car, so there's no need to differentiate it from any others.

2. Statement (a) contains a split infinitive. Do not insert an adverb between the word "to" and its verb, in this case, "study."

3. The subject of the sentence is the minimum age, and it is singular. The verb must be in agreement and must be singular as well: "Is there a minimum age for voting in the United States?"

4. It is considered poor grammar to add qualifiers such as "very," "pretty," or "rather." It makes the reader feel that you are rather or pretty or very unsure of what word to use. So, they think you are indecisive or a lightweight when it comes to a command of vocabulary.

5. In sentence (b), it is clearer who is speaking and it is clearer what "we shall see."

6. No foreign language terms, please. That's the grammarian's rule. I, for one, have stopped using *a priori* completely and replaced it with "proceeding from a known or experimental assumption." Oh well!

7. "Every body" means every physical body or every corpse—use "everybody" when you mean every person.

8. After the word "if" always use "were," so the corrected sentence would read: "If I were the president, all Americans would have health insurance now." And, a creditable and laudable sentiment this is, I might add.

9. Redundancies! In the first case, it is irrelevant—even supernumerary—to describe an innovation as new. An innovation is, *a priori*—oops, sorry—I mean by definition, new. And, guess when 8 a.m. is universally understood to occur? That's right, in the morning.

Tropes

1. Use figures of speech (tropes) sparingly, if at all. More than one in a paragraph, let alone in a sentence, is too much. One figure of speech might illuminate your meaning; two will distract the reader. The sentence, as written, has three similes. The sentence should probably have none and should read: "The golf ball landed softly on the putting green, after a smooth and accurate shot."

2. This sentence is suffering from a case of mixed metaphors, or should I say mixed metaphors and similes? Clouds and sea are combined clumsily, and then the reader is further confused by the use of a countryside metaphor. In addition, there are too many figures of speech.

3. Sentence (a) is correct. Why? Because it's Shakespeare's.

4. The answer, I hope, is as obvious to you as to any reader. It is a clumsy analogy. The gardener and the surgeon do indeed both cut and trim and tie, nonetheless it strains credibility to compare the two occupations because they involve radically different endeavors. Gardening and surgery are different in purpose and, perhaps, in their nobility as a calling. Never be clumsy in writing.

5. Grizzlies look anything but desperate when catching salmon. They just stand in the water and scoop the jumping fish into their mouths. A little patience and their meal will come to them. The simile is 180 degrees wrong. The writer meant to indicate desperate foraging for nourishment and instead made the opposite point.

Punctuation

1. Sentence (c) is correct. If a noun ends in an "s," then the apostrophe is inserted after the final "s" and another "s" is added.

2. The correct answer is (b). The clause "unless you are in a hurry" is parenthetical. Yes, these words could be in parentheses. A good, but not completely reliable, test is to see if the words can safely be left out of the sentence without radically changing the meaning. In this case the sentence, "the best way to see Vermont is on foot," stands well without the qualifier.

3. Peter walked on, his head a little higher than usual.

4. The accused, said the judge, is mad.

5. Sentence (c) is correct. If a list of nouns is about to follow, then a colon is the correct punctuation mark. By the way, battles have raged in editing rooms all over the English-speaking world as to whether the comma in a list before the "and" such as the one after "Harry" is necessary. For your purposes, it is.

A FINAL PIECE OF ADVICE

As well as the dictionaries, the encyclopedias, and the thesaurus, which I am confident you already have next to your piece of paper or computer (they are invaluable tools to anyone who wishes to write), I heartily recommend that you buy some reference material on grammar and punctuation. I recommend *Grammatically Correct* by Anne Stilman and the evergreen *Elements of Style* by Strunk and White.

CHAPTER EIGHT

The SAT Essay

As you most certainly know by now, as part of the SAT, you will be asked to write an essay in answer to a prompt. **You must address the issue raised by the prompt** in order to receive a score. Put another way, if you do not address the issue raised in the prompt you will receive a zero score. You would be surprised to find out how many students mistakenly answer the question they thought was raised by the prompt. So Golden Rule #1 is: **Always read the prompt several times to ensure that you understand it fully**.

The examiners—or readers, as the College Board calls them—are trained to measure three skills:

1. How well you develop your point of view on the topic raised by the prompt

2. How well you use reason (logic) and evidence (prior knowledge from reading) to support or prove your point of view

3. How good your writing style is—is it clear, concise, accurate, and somewhat varied?

As I have emphasized in other chapters in this book, practice is very important. If you are in the examination room reading a prompt and writing about it, and this is the first time you have ever tried to do this in the form of an essay, your chances of scoring well are low. So Golden Rule #2 is: **Practice writing timed essays, then practice again, and practice some more.**

ETS (Educational Testing Service) scores SAT essays for the College Board on a scale of 1 to 6. Two readers will read your work, and then an average of their scores is calculated. However, if the scoring difference between the two readers is more than 1 point, a third reader is called in.

The scoring is **holistic.** This means that the whole of the essay is considered, especially how well the parts make up an authentic whole. If the whole message of your essay is greater than the sum of its parts, then your chances of scoring well are greatly improved.

A perfect score is, of course, **6.** This means the work is **outstanding** and shows that you, the author, have **clear and consistent mastery** over your material. In order for this to be demonstrated, you must state your point of view on the subject suggested by the prompt and effectively and insightfully develop it. You must show by your writing that you have good critical thinking skills and use logic and appropriate examples of facts, anecdotes, and perhaps quotations—with the name of the person you are quoting or the source of a fact—to prove your point.

There has already been some controversy in the 2005 SAT essay grading. It has been reported in the press that the readers (examiners) did not deduct points for the incorrect use of "facts." Even if this is the case, keep in mind that college admissions directors may read your essay online; they are unlikely to be favorably impressed by your use of "fake facts." So, please only state something to be a fact if you can prove it with a date or some other evidence.

The perfect essay must be well-organized, clear, and coherent, with a smooth progression of ideas. Your use of language must be appropriate and definitely not mundane. In other words, your language must be apt and accurate, but also varied. Sentences should vary in length (to avoid monotonous reading) and should also be largely free of mistakes. Furthermore, you should practice the use of words, such as "furthermore," and phrases, such as "in addition to," that join thoughts together smoothly. They are known as transition words and phrases and are of immense value in making your style more fluid. So, learn them.

The next best score is a score of **5**, which means that the work is **effective** (not outstanding), and you have a **reasonably consistent mastery** of essay writing, instead of a clear and consistent mastery. To score a 5, you must still show good organization, as well as good vocabulary and language skills. Your work must be generally free of grammatical errors.

A description of a score of **4** uses words such as **competent** and **adequate** instead of effective and consistent.

A score of **3** means that the readers find the essay to be **inadequate**, with only a **developing mastery** of the skills required.

A score of **2** means that the readers find the work of the writer **seriously limited** with **little mastery** demonstrated. It means that mistakes were made, in that the point of view is vague and not clearly developed, which shows weak critical thinking skills. The essay is probably vague and perhaps incoherent, with a poor progression of ideas. The vocabulary is limited or, worse still, inaccurate. The grammar and sentence structure demonstrate little or no mastery of writing skills.

A score of **1** is even worse, of course, and the College Board uses terms such as **fundamentally lacking, no mastery,** and **seriously flawed.** There is no point of view stated, and organization, sentence structure, and grammar are very poor.

A score of **zero** means that the examinee did not answer the question at all or wrote so illegibly that no one could decipher it.

WRITING THE 25-MINUTE SAT ESSAY

Most of the other chapters in this book are devoted to detailed instructions on how to master, through constant practice, the skills of essay writing, assuming that you have plenty of time and also the companionship of others. These chapters include details on the steps needed to discover your point of view on a subject, how to develop that point of view—or thesis, or controlling idea—and how to develop and disclose your thesis in the form of an essay. In the SAT examination room, you are alone and you have only 25 minutes. It is, therefore, vital that you master the art of essay writing, by learning and practicing the principles outlined in this book *well before* you have to write your SAT essay.

Just as in sports, there are two types of essay events: sprints and distance events. The SAT essay is a sprint. The College Application essay is a distance event. Most of the chapters in this book describe how to learn to write an essay with few, if any, time limits. That is the way javelin and discus throwers, weight lifters, and sprinters train. They take plenty of time to hone their techniques and become fit, so that when the time comes, and they only have a few seconds to swim, run, throw, or lift and give it their best, they are well prepared to perform in what might be called a controlled explosion.

The woman who runs the 100-meter sprint at the Olympics has already run miles and miles over years and years, done drills, warmed up, worked on flexibility, and looked at videos dissecting her form—looking for errors and room for improvement. She has also done all this with the help of a coach.

The same could be said for training for the SAT essay. You need to practice the techniques described in this book, do warm ups, practice writing, and then dissect it and try and try again. Discuss your efforts with friends and teachers, and then try again and again and again. This way, when you go into the examination room with only 25 minutes in which to do your best, in a controlled explosion, you will be prepared.

Your aim is to do **effective, even outstanding work** that shows **consistent mastery** of your subject through **clear, well-organized, even insightful writing** that pleases the reader with its **smooth progression of ideas.**

How to Begin

It's what you do before writing that will give you the best chance of creating a work that merits a rating of 5 or 6. **Devoting 5 minutes to planning before you begin to write will make all the difference.**

I cannot stress enough the need to study the chapters in this book that cover the process of *discovery* of a point of view and the *disclosure* of that point of view through writing. This is the equivalent of training your mind for the explosive event, just like athletes train and condition their minds and bodies for the 100-meter dash.

The main thing that you *must* do before writing, and right after reading the prompt several times, is to talk it over. That raises the question, with whom do you talk when you are in an examination room? The answer is yourself, of course. That's right, talk it over with yourself (in your head—not aloud). How else will you be able to arrive at a point of view? It's called thinking.

Elsewhere in the book, I write about the fact that we alone on the planet are self-aware. Among other things, that means we can hold a debate with ourselves. People who obviously talk to themselves are frequently shunned in society. I suppose it's a matter of degree and exclusivity. If people only talk to themselves and do so incessantly, then perhaps they might need help. However, the fact that you can and do hold conversations inside your brain is not a sign of your being maladjusted—far from it, you are simply taking advantage of a gift. There are two sides to your brain and not only can you communicate between them, you *should.* In fact, you can't avoid it. It's a question of controlling or managing the conversation, so that you can quickly and efficiently arrive at a point of view on any given subject.

The point of all this is that you will instinctively and automatically ask—and answer—a number of questions about the prompt staring up at you from the SAT Test Booklet as you read it. All humans can do this.

The source of all this is your "adaptive unconscious." I would like to mention again the book "Blink" by Malcolm Gladwell, that is at the top of the *New York Times* best seller list as I write this book. This highly praised book shows you why you should generally trust your instincts. Gladwell says that if you see a truck bearing down on you, you don't raise the issue to the level of consciousness and debate outcomes or scenarios, you run. To think the predicament over consciously would mean death or injury. My version of this process involves a carton of foul-smelling milk. Do you enter into a discussion about whether to drink this poison before tossing it away? Of course not—your immune system immediately prompts you to get rid of it. Similarly, when we see any new proposition or concept we instinctively get hunches, thoughts, ideas, questions, or intuitions. We can't help it, because we're human. These instincts and hunches are probably not all valid, but—and here is essence of the method—they are all worth noting down. An idea that is invalid can be written into the essay and then triumphantly destroyed to prove or at least emphasize your point of view. So, even bad ideas are worth recording.

Asking Questions

Having written the ideas that come to mind on your work sheet, you must now ask and answer some formulaic questions. These questions will help you bring to the surface all the knowledge you have about the topic.

An essay is a blend of information that you already have—and perhaps did not know you had—and new information that you can discover, using these questions. The secret is to get as much knowledge down on paper, in the form of notes, as quickly as possible so that you can blend these into a thesis (point of view) and disclose them to your reader in a smooth, readable essay. This is mastery.

The formulaic questions are simple:

1. Who is affected most by the issues raised by this prompt?

2. **What** do the important words in this prompt mean? And what other words mean the same thing? What does the topic mean to me, my family or my country?

3. **Why** is it important to answer the issues raised by this prompt?

4. **Where** does the issue raised by this prompt have the most impact?

5. **When** does this issue become more or less important?

Now, turn the prompt into a question, unless it is already a question, and answer it. If the topic to be discussed is "Money is the root of all evil," ask yourself, "Is money the root of all evil?" This will certainly prompt ideas.

Perhaps you have heard that the tried and true formula for a debater is as follows:

1. Tell them what you are going to say.

2. Say it.

3. Tell them what you have just said.

Watch an experienced politician in a debate, and he or she will do just that. It is also a good formula for the actual writing of an essay. Tell them what you believe, say it, and then wrap it up by telling them what you have just said.

There's just one problem, and it's a big one. What is it that you believe? What is your point of view on, say, "the merits of school uniforms" or "the relative merits of democracy?" How do you discover, in 5 minutes, your point of view? (Only then can you tell your readers what you believe.) It is a truism in writing that readers can tell immediately if the point of view they are reading is authentic, or if the author simply wrote until he or she finished writing 250 words.

The freewriting of responses to the Who?, What?, Why?, Where?, and When? questions are a good beginning. Turning the prompt into a question and freewriting the response is another excellent way to help form an opinion. It will almost invariably trigger a response from your adaptive unconscious. "Is there merit in having school uniforms?" "Is democracy the best form of government?" "Is capital punishment ever merited?" Ideas will come to mind. Write them down and don't worry about penmanship, grammar, and spelling at this point—just get your ideas recorded on paper.

These ideas should not constitute a final point of view yet. In using this method, you may still come back to your first instinct about any given topic. However, if you are methodical about addressing the issue, you will sound more authentic in your essay, which is, after all, an effort to support your point of view. Who knows, you might even change your mind!

If you have time, and if you have room on the blank pages of your test booklet (consult with your teacher first to make sure you know ahead of time how much space for notes there is in the test booklet), it is a good idea to look for themes that might emerge from your freewriting. Time permitting, you might explore the prompt by using a spider diagram.

Again, I stress that the more thought that goes into an essay before writing, the better your chances of doing **effective, even outstanding work** that shows **consistent mastery** of your subject. The more thought that goes into an essay, the more **insightful** a reader is going to believe you are. The more thought that goes into an essay, the easier it is going to be to write in a **clear, well-organized**, and **smooth** style.

Of course the only way to make sure that you will be ready on the day is to practice discovering your point of view and disclosing it until it is second nature. A sprinter's technique—out of the blocks, sprinting, and finishing—is never a work in progress on the big day. It is second nature.

CONCLUSION

In this book, I have been following the framework of the 250- to 350-word, five-paragraph essay. I have several reasons for doing this. First, by following my prewriting and writing methods and practicing them regularly, you have a better chance to discover your point of view and to disclose it with a greater sense of confidence and authenticity. If you are familiar with a technique, it becomes easier to follow.

However, your SAT essay is not exactly like the sprint analogy I used earlier. In a sprint, you are told where to start, where to end, and within which lane you must stay. Few of the essay examples that are reproduced on the SAT Web site are 250- to 350-word, five-paragraph essays. Some of the essays may contain only two larger paragraphs or one large and a couple of smaller ones.

You may prefer a more free-form approach to the actual writing or disclosing of your point of view. If this is the case, note my description of the bull's-eye paragraph in Chapter 6 of the book. This is a technique where the final paragraph of the essay is written first, and the rest of the essay becomes an argument leading up to that paragraph and its conclusions. You are not told where to begin, where to end, or the path that you must follow.

You should be clear that, no matter what your approach or format, your essay must **demonstrate consistent mastery of your subject and be effective, insightful, clear, organized, and smooth.** It is possible to do this in any format. If you are like me, you will do better with a structure such as the five-paragraph essay, particularly with a tight time limit.

CHAPTER NINE

The ACT Essay

As you are aware, you will be asked to write an essay as part of your ACT Assessment. This book's approach to essay writing involves two distinct phases: thinking your way to *discovering* a point of view about a given topic and *disclosing* that point of view in an essay.

In the book, there are many examples of how to carry out this entire process in groups, with plenty of time, and how to do this alone, again with plenty of time. This chapter is devoted to the task that faces those taking the ACT—how to do this in 30 minutes.

First, let's start by identifying the rubrics—rules and directions—that will govern evaluation of the essay part of your examination. If you do not know the rules of the game, it makes it much harder to play.

The golden rule for test-takers in any examination is: "Always answer the question asked, not the one you think is being asked." The best way to avoid the costly error of answering the wrong question is to carefully read the question several times.

The ACT essay is examined holistically. This means that, although you will be evaluated on individual tasks such as using correct grammar, it is the overall impression that your essay creates from all its elements that is the most important consideration.

Two specially trained readers will read your essay. They will also award points for your effort, from 1 (low) to 6 (high). Your writing sub-score is the sum of the two readers' assessments. This sub-score ranges from 2 (low) to 12 (high). If there is a discrepancy of more than a point between the grades of the two readers, then a third judge is brought in to resolve the final score.

Here are five pointers that should always be in your mind when writing an essay:

1. Show the reader of your work that you are mature enough in your thinking to take a position on a topic, or prompt, and defend it.

2. Show the reader of your work that you can maintain focus on that topic throughout your essay.

3. Show your reader that you can expand on the topic or prompt by the use of logic, reason, and supporting ideas.

4. Show your reader that you can organize your thoughts and ideas in a logical and consistent manner.

5. Show your reader that you can use Standard Written English to communicate your message clearly and effectively.

Here are a few specifics on the ACT scoring:

- Papers that score **6 and 5** are considered **upper-range.** A score of 6 is **Exceptional.** A score of 5 is **Competent.**
- Papers that score **4 and 3** are considered **mid-range.** A score of 4 is **adequate.** A score of 3 shows **developing skills.**
- Papers that score **2 and 1** are considered **lower-range.** A score of 2 is **inconsistent** or **weak.** A score of 1 shows **little** or **no skill.**

Obviously, a score of 6 is the most desirable, and here are the criteria for achieving that goal:

❏ You must respond to the prompt.

❏ You must take a clear position on the issue identified in the prompt.

❑ You must demonstrate a clear understanding of the issue and its complexities.

❑ Your ideas must be fully explored and elaborated upon in an ample, specific, and logical manner.

❑ You must maintain a clear focus throughout the essay.

❑ Your introductory sentence must be clear and unambiguous.

❑ Your concluding sentences must neatly summarize the essay.

❑ Transitions between ideas must be smoothly executed.

❑ Sentence structure must vary.

❑ Errors, such as grammatical errors, logic errors, and spelling mistakes, must be few and should not distract the reader.

The essay may follow a predictable format such as the 250- to 350-word, five-paragraph essay, or it may be more free-flowing. Either way, it must be cohesive and authentic (your true voice).

The difference between an **exceptional** execution of all the points above in an essay that scores a 6, and the **competent** essay that scores a 5, is in the eyes of the beholders, namely the readers of your work.

To give you a score of 5, the readers will be looking at how well you measure up in all of the categories outlined above. How well did you respond to the prompt? Did you engage the issue raised by the prompt? Did you show that you understood the issue? Did you explore all issues of the prompt and its implications? Did you explore your ideas on the prompt amply, specifically, and logically? Were you focused during the essay? Did your introductory sentence announce a belief, and did your summary sentences wrap up your argument? Did you use transitions to create a smooth flow and did you vary your sentence structure, showing a good command of English? Did you avoid grammatical errors and was your logic sound? Whatever format you used for your essay, was it cohesive and authentic?

If, in the reader's opinion, you showed only **competent** skills in most of these areas, which by the way is nothing to be ashamed of, then you will probably get a 5. It takes a lot of work and ability to decide on a position, show a clear understanding of the material, evaluate the implications of your position, be specific in writing about and defending your position, be consistent and focused throughout, and keep it all basically error-free.

If the readers of your work see only **adequate** skills in these areas of competence then you will score a 4, again nothing to be ashamed of.

If they see that you are **developing some** of these skills, they will score you as a 3. If you are **weak** or **inconsistent** in your grasp of the elements of essay writing, then they will give you a score of 2. If, in their opinion, you have **inadequate, little**, or **no** skills, then the score will be 1.

WRITING THE 30-MINUTE ACT ESSAY

How is it possible to decide on a position, having carefully read a prompt, demonstrate a clear understanding of your material, fully explore your ideas, elaborate on them in a logical and specific manner, maintain focus, and write clearly while making few, if any, mistakes? This is difficult enough to do when you have plenty of time. So, what is the answer, or at least my answer? Practice, rehearse, train, prepare, drill; they all mean basically the same thing. Discover a routine that works for you and follow that routine again and again, until it is second nature.

How do athletes prepare for sprints? They certainly do a lot of sprinting, of course. They also do a lot of other things in order to prepare for the day when, prompted by a starter's pistol, they will run 100 or so strides down a running track as fast as they can, making the fewest mistakes and optimizing the techniques they have learned over years of preparation. They use weights, they use visualization techniques, runners swim and swimmers run, they stretch, they do yoga, they eat correctly, and so on. This is all to make sure that when the time comes to sprint, it will be second nature.

A 30-minute essay is a sprint—a mind sprint—and I believe that the only way you can be ready for the fateful examination day is to practice the techniques detailed in this book until you can get the job done in the time frame allotted. I recommend practicing these techniques both in groups and alone. Of course, it helps to have a goal. An athlete going into a competition without a goal in mind is not likely to achieve much above average performance. If the athlete's goal is just to finish the 100-meter sprint and cross the finish line in a vertical position, regardless of time or position, then to describe this goal as modest is an understatement.

You have read the requirements for the grading system of 1 through 6. Only you can realistically decide what is possible. Nevertheless, don't aim too low. Discuss your strengths and weaknesses with a teacher, parent, or friend. Don't forget that the grading is holistic. If you are weak on grammar and strong on staying focused, one can make up for the other. Look at all of the criteria that the ACT readers scrutinize before giving a score. Now, honestly rate yourself on a scale of 1 to 10 on each one. Use the help of teachers or parents. Don't ask friends, however—they might only wish to give you good or optimistic grades in order to make you feel good or to get the same favor in return. The truth is your friend.

There are two parts to an essay. Perhaps I should say there are two activities that you must do, and do well, in order to score in the upper range. The first part is the discovery part. **This is what you must do before beginning to write.** It is the part where you follow a formula that will help you discover how you feel about the issue raised in the prompt. If you don't do this and simply begin writing, what will you write about?

As far as I can see, nowhere are the readers for both ACT and SAT asked to look for a quality called authenticity. However, the sum total of their holistic view of your essay does imply that they are looking for an authentic voice; one that is expressed very well. So, how do you find your voice, your truthful opinion on a subject raised in the essay prompt? Furthermore, how can you find out what you believe about the issue in 5 minutes, which is about all the time you can devote to this exercise, leaving you 25 minutes in which to write your essay?

First of all, 25 minutes is quite a reasonable amount of time to write 250 to 350 words, especially if you have a really clear idea about the subject matter. If you have no ideas or opinions to express, 25 minutes is an eternity. If you have multiple opinions, or poorly conceived opinions, 25 minutes is no time at all.

Here is what I suggest as a framework for practice sessions. **After you have read all the chapters in this book, train yourself to be able to go through the following routines until they become second nature.**

1. Read the prompt several times to make absolutely sure that you understand what it is saying. Read it aloud if you can—you will be surprised how well that works in terms of accurately getting the point from the paper into your head.

2. Next, talk to yourself (in your head, not aloud). Discuss the topic. Elsewhere in this book I have already discussed the fact that one of the most distinguishing characteristics of humanity is that we *can* talk to ourselves. We can hold a discussion as if we were two persons, not one. I don't know about you, but I'm very glad I can talk to myself, and I do. I use both sides of my brain.

3. Write your ideas down as soon as they start coming. Check with your teacher about how much space you have in your test booklet to use for designing your essay. At this point, there are no bad ideas, just ideas. Use the freewriting technique to capture all your hunches, instincts, speculations, ideas, and suggestions, which come, according to author and researcher Malcolm Gladwell, from your "adaptive unconscious." They are to be trusted just as much as carefully-thought-out, conscious ideas, because both are speculative in nature.

4. An essay is a mixture of information that you already have—and perhaps do not yet know that you have—and information that you can gather about the topic. In thinking about the topic and freewriting, you are releasing thoughts and knowledge that you already have about the

subject. Now you must ask some questions about the topic that will help you gain more information, or insights, into the question. These are the Who?, What?, Why?, Where?, and When? questions. They are critical, so memorize them.

5. **Who** is affected most by the issue raised in the prompt?

6. **What** do the key words in the prompt mean?

7. **Why** is this issue important?

8. **Where** does this issue have the most impact?

9. **When** does—or did—the issue become important?

Now, turn the prompt into a question. If it already is a question, ask it in a different way.

If you have ever been in a debate club meeting, then you are probably familiar with the mantra of debaters everywhere. "Tell them what you're going to say, say it, and then tell them what you just said." This mantra leaves out a crucial initial step, "Decide what you're going to tell them." However if you add this, the formula works quite well for an essay: "Decide what to say, tell them what you decided, say it, and then tell them what you just said."

How well you respond to a prompt, how well you take a position on the issue, how well you understand the subject matter, how focused you are on the issue, how well your first sentence states your position, and how well your last sentences summarize it are all criteria readers look for. Doing these things well will result in high marks, and I am absolutely convinced that the better you are at spending productive time *before* writing, the better your grades will be. The only way to become more productive in using the few minutes before writing is practice, practice, practice. Practice thinking about the subject and practice coming up with an authentic point of view. The only way to become good at the writing part—disclosing your point of view—again is to practice. Remember, the readers want the essay to flow smoothly, they want to see few, if any, mistakes, and good, varied sentence structure. How can you give the readers what they want? Well, a gymnast learns what the judges are looking for and gives it to them by learning and practicing the rules of the sport. You need to learn what the readers are looking for and practice, practice, practice the rules of good essay writing. are in the wealthiest nations. These companies claim that the drugs can only be produced if they are protected by patents, and that they must be funded by the high profit margins made by selling the drugs and vaccines in the wealthiest countries. There is little or no incentive for the drug companies of Europe and America to create drugs to treat diseases that mostly affect the Third World.

CONCLUSION

Now you continue and, of course, remember that in order to score a 6, you must strive to demonstrate **competent**, even **exceptional**, skills in communicating that you have a **clear understanding** of the issue and its complexities. Your ideas must be **fully explored** and **elaborated** upon. Your style must be **clear** and **logical.** You must **focus** on your **thesis**, or point of view, throughout your essay. The essay must be **organized.** Your first sentence must state your **opinion**, and your last sentence must **tell your reader what you have just proved**, or at least written. Your motto might be: No banalities, no inanities. Be lucid, organized, smooth, and focused.

CHAPTER TEN

The College Admissions Essay

Instructions from colleges for the entrance application essay generally limit essay length to 250 to 500 words. The time available for writing your essay is limited only by the application deadline, and the 1-3-1 structure may not necessarily be useful. The following are examples of topic choices from the Common Application Form used by many colleges.

- Indicate a person who has had a significant influence on you, and describe that influence.
- Describe a character in fiction, an historical figure, or a creative work, as in art, literature, music, or science that has had an influence on you, and explain that influence.
- Evaluate a significant achievement or risk that you have taken or an ethical dilemma that you have faced and its impact upon you.
- Discuss some issue of a personal, local, national, or international concern and its impact on you.
- A topic of your own choice.

The first four topics contain the word "you" in the prompt. There is a reason for this. The colleges cannot possibly interview all applicants face-to-face. The essay acts in place of the interview. It is your representative, your delegate, your proxy—your chance to tell the admissions director who you are.

The issue of national importance or the person who influenced you is of secondary importance to the admissions directors. What they want—in fact need—to know is why they should accept you instead of the other 4 to 9 applicants who are competing with you for a place at their college.

The admissions committee knows that your SAT verbal and math scores are only a predictor of your ability to learn and memorize. They also know—and I have spoken to many—that the essay is their only chance to see how you think and how you communicate ideas. They want answers to the following questions: Who is this person? Is she authentic? Is he a person of integrity?

As I have said repeatedly, make no mistake about it, you are the subject of your essay. This, of course, raises the fundamental question: Do you know who you are? No doubt, you read this question and reacted with an exasperated and quite normal response: "Of course I know who I am." If you are absolutely certain that you already know yourself well enough to be able to confidently transmit—in writing—your personal philosophy to a total stranger, who will make a life-altering decision about your future without ever consulting you beyond reading your essay, then read no further. If on the other hand, like the vast majority of us, you do not yet know enough about yourself and would like to find out more, then read on.

DISCOVERING YOU

The prevailing opinion among parents and teachers is that teenagers are notorious for knowing everything and thinking that they are immortal. I remember being just like that when I was a teen. To the dismay of family and teachers alike, I was convinced that I knew better than anyone else did, and I also had no fear of death. In other words, I was a typical teenager.

The sad truth is that none of us is either all-knowing or facing a life without end. Accepting this truth is a good start, because the inquiry into our own nature is a lifelong and, as I have discovered, very fulfilling enterprise. Imagine what it must have been like to live before people began to ask questions such as "Who am I?" "What sort of world was it before anyone looked at the earth, sea, and sky and asked 'How did this all come about?'" "How many times did people attempt to answer these fundamental questions before their findings were recorded and preserved?"

Fortunately for us, some of the greatest thinkers who have ever lived, men with names such as Socrates, Plato, and Aristotle, did record their process of discovery. Their answers have been preserved and, like all great ideas, they are simple, and they still hold sway in the twenty-first century. It pays to know a little about these ideas.

The word "idea" today has a different meaning from the one understood in classical Greece. Two and a half millennia ago, an idea meant a unique picture that identified something for what it was. The idea of Socrates or you is unmistakably that of, you guessed it, Socrates or you. It is a different idea from all other "ideas." It sets things apart. The idea that other people form of you may well be different than the idea you have formed of yourself. This is the basis for the common complaint we have when addressing authority figures: "You just don't understand me." Does that sound familiar?

Discovering an accurate and honest idea of yourself is a necessary first step in writing an essay. Listen carefully to what follows and you will perhaps find out how to go about discovering the idea that is uniquely you. This process will help you to understand who you are, to communicate that idea to others, and to comprehend a little better why others react to you the way they do.

Aristotle went one step further than his predecessors did. He concluded that not only are all objects "ideas"—a better word today might be "concepts"—he also proposed that ideas have two components. They have a **form,** or shape, and a **substance,** which today we might call content. The combination of these two attributes—let's use modern terminology, shape and content—gives the idea its identity. The combination of your external shape and your internal content gives you your identity. If you know what they are, you know who you are. If one or other is absent—or different—the identity changes. Each pebble on the beach is unique and, under the microscope, each snowflake is certainly distinct from the next one. Each pebble, snowflake, and human being has a shape and a content that makes it uniquely identifiable as an idea.

Around 2,200 years after the classical Greeks made their amazing philosophical discoveries about identity, an Englishman named Herbert Spencer proposed that our substance, or content, could also be separated into two parts: a **conscious intellect** and an **unconscious will.** He wondered which was more important and decided it must be the will, since it is not the intellect that pushes the heart to beat. He concluded also that the will shapes the brain to know as surely as it shapes the hand to grasp. So there you have it! Your shape and your content determine the idea that is you. Your content is comprised of a conscious intellect and an unconscious will. Your shape is a result of heritage and environment. (Try debating all this with a friend.) You should know something else about yourself: your desire to learn is born in you. DNA research suggests that many genes enable human speech, cognition, and language.

Let's talk about "identity" a bit more. Look around you—the shapes, or forms, that humans take are infinitely varied. Their substance, or content, is just as varied. No two humans are alike, not even identical twins. The intellectual descendants of those ancient Greeks and Spencer are called psychologists. They now define identity in this way: "The distinguishing characteristics of an individual are as follows: who we are, what our roles are, and what our capabilities are." Not much of an improvement on the efforts of the Greeks, but there you have it.

To me, one of the most confusing, contradictory, and oxymoronic characteristics of the human race is the fact that we are the only species on Earth who are capable of thinking our way to an understanding of who we are, and yet so few of us try. We are capable of introspection, of contemplating our own thoughts and self, and of self-examination. The message of this book is to use that gift. As I have said, the act of writing is a process of learning about ourselves. Writing an essay is like gazing into a mirror and frankly accepting the honest portrayal we see there. This ability is the gift of human freedom; we can either allow it to intimidate us, or we can use it to our advantage. I leave it to you to decide which of these I recommend.

If you do not try to understand who you are and to communicate that discovery, then the college admissions officer, and later your boss, will decide who you are instead. Do you want that? Ask yourself whether you wish to define yourself in the eyes of others, or have others define you.

It is important to understand that you cannot fail to communicate your shape, or form, unless you are in disguise every time you are in the presence of others. You should also understand that you cannot avoid communicating your substance, or content. You do this with every gesture, word, or written communication. If you find out who you are first, then other people will have a better chance to know the real you and will not make up their minds without your active involvement. **This is clearly to your advantage.** The atoms and elements in your body are identical to those found in our sun's core. You are a child of the stars. You are a cosmic being. You are also unique. You are one of a kind. You are special. There is only one "idea" that is you. Find it!

Try this: Put yourself in context first, just as you would with any topic. As you do, freewrite the ideas that come to you.

➤ What are you part of? The human race.

➤ What is humanity a part of? The animal kingdom.

➤ What is the animal kingdom a part of? Life on Earth.

➤ What is Earth a part of? The universe.

On the next page, draw a diagram with yourself at the center. Put yourself in context by first diagramming "thinking up." Now, begin to break yourself down by asking, "Of all the untold trillions of entities in the universe, what makes me unique?"

Your Diagram

YOU

Start by asking the important questions to which you know the answers, such as your ethnicity or gender, economic status, nationality, and age. Perhaps you could even discover some of your most outstanding characteristics. Here is a checklist where you can indicate some of the characteristics that apply to you.

- ❑ Selfless
- ❑ A Loner
- ❑ Smart
- ❑ Submissive
- ❑ Tough-minded
- ❑ Practical
- ❑ A Risk-Taker
- ❑ Relaxed
- ❑ Adventurous
- ❑ Suspicious
- ❑ Shrewd
- ❑ Tense
- ❑ Self-sufficient
- ❑ Controlling
- ❑ Sociable
- ❑ Reserved
- ❑ Emotional
- ❑ Dominant
- ❑ Trusting
- ❑ Conservative
- ❑ Uncontrolled

❏ Conscientious

❏ Sensitive

❏ Imaginative

❏ Apprehensive

❏ Controlled

Be honest with yourself, ask others who know you well, and think before you pick any of these characteristics. Next, ask questions that seem less important, such as your preferred style of clothing, friends, or activities. What are your dislikes? Just how smart are you? Are you good at some subjects and not others? Finally work up your courage and honestly answer the questions about why you like, prefer, hate, or dislike something or someone. No one else has to see your answers, but it is a productive exercise. Do it again and again over time and you will find yourself changing. If you ignore your own self, then others will ask these questions about you and answer them themselves—and those answers will probably not always be to your liking. By getting to know who you are, you are in a position to influence your future. Others will constantly ask these questions about you; shouldn't you ask them of yourself?

The teenage period, or adolescence, as some call it, is characterized by an unconscious search for identity and one's role in life. Since others need to know your identity in order to make decisions about you and your future, you need to make a conscious effort to discover your identity and understand it.

There is a tension in all of us in the teenage years; more so than in other life periods. This is not surprising since teens are torn between being dependent on others and yet wanting to be independent. There is also tension between a teen's need to conform and a need to assert uniqueness. Teens are looking for the role they will play in society. Learning something about themselves is a very good start.

College admissions people, teachers, and parents all understand this. Believe it or not, they all went through it—adolescence, I mean. They know that you are changing, that the child is becoming the adult. Change is the only constant during high school. The college people want to know how well you are coping with it. It will come through in your writing, so know yourself. Ask the questions. Who am I? What am I? Why am I the way I am? Where do I belong? What is it that I don't know about myself and should? We are shaped by our responses to the inevitable changes we experience. This is particularly true during the teenage years when a blueprint is still unfolding. You are descendants of the past and parents of the future; you are humanity's immortality; since, if you all choose not to have children, humanity will die out.

Biologists see us as a collection of organs. Organs for motion, nutrition, reproduction, perception, and thought. You know that you are more than just a sum of all these parts. That is the secret you must uncover and pass on to others. The college admissions people know all this; it is only fair that you should also.

PRACTICE EXAMPLE

More than one hundred eleventh- and twelfth-grade students at Pineview, Booker, and Lakewood Ranch High Schools on Florida's west coast helped me by reviewing and critiquing this book. Many suggested that they would like to see an example of how to write a college admissions essay, using the methods of discovery that I have outlined in previous chapters. Here is one.

essay

Describe an historical character who has had an influence on you, and explain that influence.

Where do we begin? Well, an historical character limits the choice to men or women who lived in a previous age. So, that eliminates some of one's first choices such as aunts and uncles, teachers, or grandparents (unless they were of historical significance).

My first suggestion is that there are two words in the essay topic that should be examined carefully and that will help you discover your authentic point of view on this topic. The first word is "you," and the second word is "influence."

Examining these two words in context will help you decide who really did exert an influence on you, rather than thinking of a person whom you admired. Just because you admired them does not necessarily mean that they exerted an influence on you. However, by looking at the words carefully, you will be able to check and see if your instinctive choice for the honor of most influential historical figure deserves the title.

Earlier in this chapter, you examined yourself in context. The following diagram is an abbreviated version of my fictitious essay author examining herself.

Diagram V

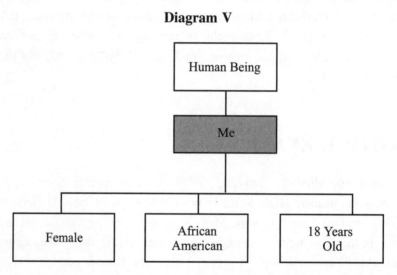

So, now is the time to examine and diagram the other important word in the essay topic—"influence." Here's what I did: Once again with the aid of a dictionary, I began to build a contextual view of the word. As I did, ideas came to me and I wrote them down. I read the definition of the word "influence": "A power to indirectly affect a person or a course of events." From another source, I discovered that the word "influence" is defined as the "effect produced by that power." This power obviously causes change. But what is influence? It's an attribute, I decided.

The following is the result of this *Thinking Around the Box*™. The first part was the diagram and then the ideas that occurred as I was diagramming. Of course, I made sure to ask the Who?, What?, Why?, Where?, and When? questions.

Diagram W

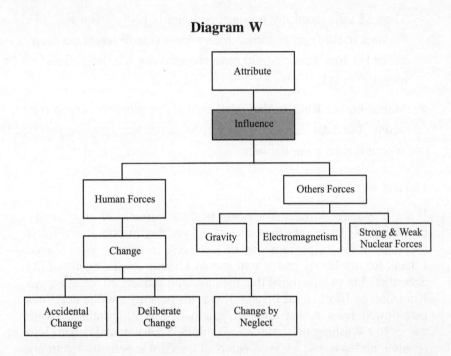

Thoughts:

➤ The essay is about historical figures, so the bits of the diagram about gravity and so on don't count. They influence me fundamentally of course, but not in the way the essay question indicates.

➤ Human forces are always in play. Like everyone else, I have been influenced by the decisions made by historical figures. I had never thought before about whether these historical figures made these decisions deliberately, accidentally, or by neglect.

➤ I think that deliberate decisions, or policy decisions as they are now called, made a greater difference to me than changes that occurred by neglect or accident.

➤ I am African-American. What human forces influenced me most?

➤ The Europeans who traded in human cargo; the American plantation owners; the African tribal leaders who profited in the slave trade; the American and European politicians.

➤ They all influenced my personal and family history. But who made the decisions? If an historical figure had made different decisions in his or her life, which would have changed my life most? This is a key question to ask.

➤ Martin Luther King Jr. and other civil rights pioneers helped right a wrong. But who caused the wrong, or perpetrated it, or perpetuated it? Who influenced me the most?

Here is her essay:

I am a young African-American woman coming of age at the beginning of the twenty-first century. I am free, in one of the freest societies on Earth, perhaps one of the freest in history. Who should I thank for my liberty and whom should I blame for the agony of my ancestors? I have concluded that the man who influenced me most was King George III of Great Britain. It was his insanity and the decisions that flowed from it that turned a group of English gentlemen with names like Washington, Jefferson, Franklin, Madison, and Adams into revolutionaries whose ideas of personal freedom eventually led to my ancestors' emancipation.

It was not a journey without trouble. It turned North against South. It increased discrimination along the way. Things got a lot worse before they began to get better, beginning about the time my grandfather was a young man listening to a preacher in Atlanta.

By the 1950s, King George's madness was finally beginning to make sense of the lives of my ancestors. By the end of the 1960s, the ill treatment that had been normal and accepted for my people had become illegal.

Morality begins with equal rights and must come first from people's hearts, not the law. However, if my grandparents's parents could see me now—destined for college and already taking my rightful place in society—they would be amazed, I'm sure.

So I thank the King of Hanover and England. His affliction—I read it was porphyry—caused him to make incompetent decisions, which lost him the American colonies, which in turn influenced history and led to my opportunity, and I intend to grasp it with both hands.

Now, let me be quite clear about something. I, your author, am neither black nor female, and I am certainly not 18. However, by using the techniques described in the book, I think I was able to write something imaginative that might just stand out in the piles and piles of applications stacked up on the admission director's desk.

CONCLUSION

Writing about a subject helps to develop a point of view on that subject. It also helps to develop a personal belief system. Each and every time you write, you will learn more about the world and even more about yourself. Of course, reading and thinking are important to developing knowledge; however, writing gives them both a purpose.

If you get to know yourself by reading, thinking, and writing, you will learn who you are and be able to make more informed decisions about your life and the lives of others. As I have said, others will constantly make decisions for you if you do not make them for yourself. Don't let others or yourself make decisions that affect you or a loved one that are based on inadequate information and poorly thought out.

Composing an essay is, at its heart, the process of self-discovery through critical and creative thinking—all around the box—and disclosing to others, in a stylish way, what you have found out.

CHAPTER Eleven

How It's Done

This chapter encapsulates the content presented in the book. It provides an example of each of the discovery methods described and provides linear and visual summaries of the entire essay-writing process.

EXERCISES IN DISCOVERY

Earlier in this book, I promised to give some examples of discovery—how to think your way to a point of view on any given topic. I have discussed three methods of *Thinking Around the Box*™. They are Contextual Thinking (with diagramming and freewriting), the Spider Diagram, and Lists. I have taken three essay topics and applied one method to each.

Keep this in mind: topics that are somewhat philosophical in nature are best suited to being diagrammed, using either Contextual Thinking or the Spider Diagram. Topics that are a little less profound, or even downright mundane, should generally be addressed by using Lists.

The only way to decide which method to use is practice. After you have practiced all the techniques for some period of time, it will become apparent to you which one best lends itself to a given topic.

Contextual Thinking

Topic #1 is one of those profound questions that we all need to consider: *What limits should be placed on our rights as citizens, and why?*

I brought together a small group of students to brainstorm this issue. They had all read this book and knew its methods. We decided that the key word to be diagrammed was "Rights," and that rights are part of the privileges of membership. We found this definition of rights: "A power or privilege to which one is justly entitled." We turned the essay topic into a new question: "Should any limits be placed on a citizen's rights?" We asked the Who?, What?, Why?, Where?, and When? questions. We personalized the topic by discussing how limits on certain rights would affect us as individuals, families, and members of the same school. We thought about examples of rights. I reminded them that, at this point, there are no bad ideas, no right or wrong ideas, no idea that should be rejected because it might be controversial. We wrote one idea on one piece of paper at a time and kept at it for about 10 or 15 minutes. Then, we categorized the notes and completed the diagram. Here's our work:

essay

What limits should be placed on our rights as citizens, and why?

Freewriting Notes

- Rights are balanced by obligations
- Citizenship
- Membership in clubs
- Religious membership
- Member of the military
- Privileges
- Protecting rights of other people
- Human rights
- Entitlements
- Natural law
- Freedom of speech
- Freedom of assembly
- Right to bear arms

What limits should be placed on our rights as citizens, and why?

Contextual Thinking

```
                    ┌─────────────────┐
                    │ Privileges of   │
                    │ Membership      │
                    └─────────────────┘
                    │                 │
            ┌───────────────┐   ┌──────────────┐
            │    Rights     │   │ Obligations  │
            └───────────────┘   └──────────────┘
```

Other Kinds of Memberships	Rights and Privileges of Citizenship	To Only Exercise One's Rights and Privileges as Long as They Do Not Interfere with the Rights and Privileges of Others

Religious Organizations	Clubs		Human Rights	

	Military Organizations		Individual Entitlements	

			Natural Law	

Freedoms:	
Speech	Seizure
Press	Jury Trial
Assembly	Petition
Religion	Bear Arms

Possible point of view, or thesis: "The many rights and freedoms that come with citizenship are balanced by obligations, including a commitment to protecting other people's rights."

Spider Diagram

Topic #2 is quite a profound topic, but it is hardly in the same league with the first one about citizens' rights: *Why are so many people superstitious despite advances in science?* This topic is perfect for a Spider Diagram. Here is what the group developed:

Why are so many people superstitious despite advances in science?

Spider Diagram

Stars	Cards	Tea Leaves	Palms

Fortune Telling

Search for Other Ways to Discover Mystical Side

Spiritualism (communing with the dead)

Belief that Ignores Science (occult)

Ignorance

Theory	Experiment	Proof

Science

Fear   Insecurity

Superstition

Faith in God Cannot Be Proved or Disproved

Choices

Belief	Disbelief	Agnosticism

Freewriting ideas went directly into the diagram, which effectively categorized the ideas as well. **We came up with this point of view, or thesis:** "People need to explain or have some sense of control over areas of life where science has no place; that need may be met by a spiritual faith. In the absence of faith, the occult may become a very attractive alternative." Could *you* finish this essay?

Lists

Topic #3 is perfect for the List approach: *Hats*. As soon as I mentioned this topic, someone asked, "How in the world can anyone write 250 words on a subject such as hats?" For some students, it would be tough—for others it might be the perfect topic. I stood at the whiteboard and wrote down the time of day. I told them we had 10 minutes for *Thinking Around the Box*™, in this case the hatbox. We sorted the results into categories. Below, you can see what we came up with. You might be surprised that so many ideas could result; I am not. My silly contributions were to ask if a person wearing a baseball cap backward seems to everyone (or just to me) to lose several IQ points by doing so and to ask also if wigs are hats.

Hats

List

1. Symbols of office:
   - Royalty
   - Legal profession
   - In religions
   - Military
   - Political

2. Protection against:
   - Crashes
   - Falling debris
   - Rain
   - Sun
   - Cold
   - Weapons
   - Chemicals, viruses, other hazards
   - Opponents in sports such as boxing, hockey, and baseball

3. Personal adornment:
   - Shape
   - Ornamentation

4. Camouflage

5. History:
   • From fur to armored knights to crowns to space helmets

6. Symbols of academic rank:
   • Mortar boards

7. Hats as a social statement:
   • At the horse races
   • Group affiliations

8. Ceremonial hats:
   • Serious
   • Festive

9. Gestures made with the hat:
   • Tossed in the air (celebration)
   • Doffed, tipped, touched (respect)
   • "Tossed in the ring" (joining a contest)

10. Other uses:
    • A cowboy scoops up water for his thirsty horse

11. To communicate a decision:
    • In Britain, a judge dons a black hat to signify the death sentence.
    • A veil may signify a decision about faith or a commitment.

Point of view, or thesis: As a practical person, I believe that the most important function of hats is protection. From rain, sun, and cold-weather hats to football helmets, hard hats, and the uppermost part of a moon suit, hats protect that amazing organ we all depend on—the brain.

Could *you* write an essay about hats after this kind of brainstorming? I think you could at least write a better essay than you could write without it.

START TO FINISH

Being a person with a logical turn of mind and knowing that many of the readers of this book may well have an orientation toward systems and engineering, or perhaps a graphical inclination, I decided to summarize this book with a flow chart. On the next page, you will find a flow chart that graphically steps you through my ideal process for writing an essay. Some people will find it confusing; others will find it helpful. It simply outlines the various steps I have discussed in detail in the body of this book.

For those who prefer words to diagrams, here is the material from the flow chart in a more descriptive, process analysis form:

- Examine the topic by reading it several times. Personalize it. Turn it into a question.
- As you read, freewrite (capture) your thoughts.
- Decide which method of analysis to use: Contextual Thinking (with diagramming up and down, as well as freewriting), Spider Diagram (around), or List (linear).
- Do the analysis and capture your thoughts as you do—one idea on one note.
- Sort your ideas into piles and examine them.
- Write a preliminary thesis statement (point of view).
- Decide whether to write an informative or persuasive essay.
- Decide on techniques: narration, description, illustration, process analysis, categorization, definition, comparison and contrast, and statement and proof.
- Decide how to introduce the topic: background statement, question, story, fact, or definition.
- Revisit the thesis statement and finalize it.
- Refer to the notes and write a sentence or paragraph on each idea contained. Link them by transitional words and phrases.
- Edit and polish the essay by making sure of the spelling, punctuation, flow, sentence construction, and logic.

Essay Writing Flow Chart

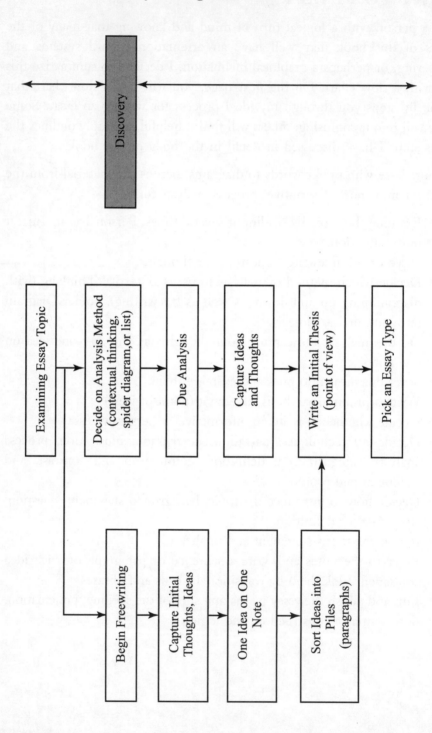

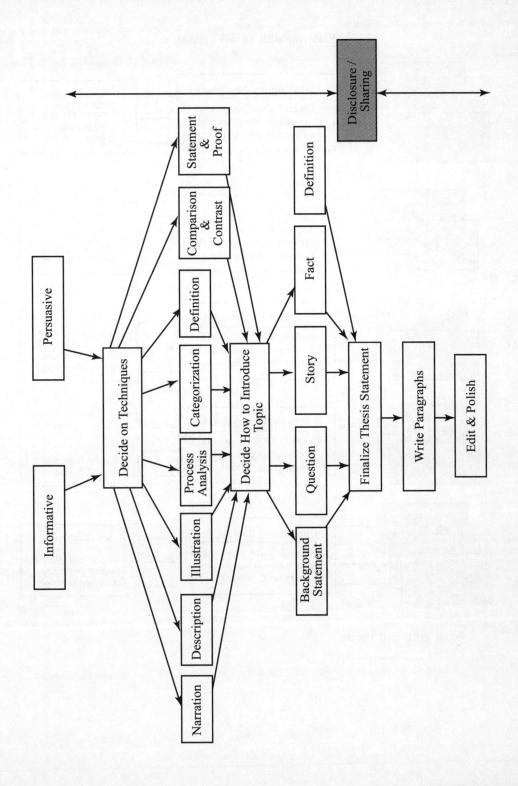

5 Paragraph (1-3-1) Essay

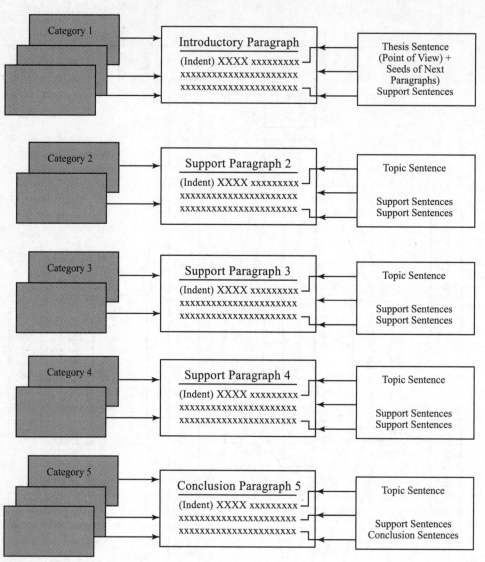

Now edit and polish.

CHAPTER TWELVE

Starting Points

Essay writing is not an end point, but a starting point. When you practice *Thinking Around the Box*™, essay writing becomes a means of self-discovery, learning, and development of yourself and your personal philosophy.

DEVELOPMENT OF LANGUAGE

This section is optional only if you already know how civilization came about and the part played in its evolution by speech and writing.

I have tried throughout this book to demonstrate the importance of setting things in a larger context, in hopes of opening your eyes to a wider world. The implicit topic of this book—other than you, the writer, of course—is language itself. Setting it in its larger context was an illuminating experience for me. I hope it is for you. So here goes!

Language, the vocal sounds and their written equivalents by which we humans make ourselves understood, is a transforming gift. It permits us to discover and to disclose. Imagine for a moment a world without language and you will see what I mean.

Long before we humans could write, we could speak. This gift of speech appears to be uniquely human; it is part of our identity. Anthropologists aren't very precise about just when humans began to speak. Some say we began gossiping sometime around 200,000 years ago, others surmise we began to talk only 40,000 years before the present time. Writing down our spoken thoughts and ideas, however, was not humanity's first non-verbal means of communicating. Artists and accountants can claim that honor. Beautiful cave art that is at least 30,000 years old exists in France and elsewhere, and we know that people in Africa carved notches on bones as a way of keeping records 25,000 years ago.

Some 5,000 years ago, the need for human speech to be recorded necessitated the invention of writing, which some have called "frozen speech." Writing appeared in several places at about the same time. Its invention was an event every bit as transformational for our ancestors as the discovery of a way to harness and control fire, and the invention of tools. Historians consider the invention of writing so important that it is called "our supreme intellectual achievement, the discovery that civilized its inventors." Historians divide a nation's history into "before writing," which they term "prehistory," and "history," which begins when a nation learns to record its thoughts.

Before writing, what was spoken was always temporary; it lasted only as long as an echo or the memory of the listener. Recording the spoken word by the use of symbols changed everything. A brief review of prehistory helps us understand how writing came into existence. For perhaps 2 million years or more, our distant ancestors roamed the forests as simple hunters and gatherers. They followed the herds and picked whatever vegetables, fruits, and nuts were at hand. The first, simple stone tools were created about 750,000 years ago. This event gave rise to the Old Stone (Paleolithic) Age.

About 10,000 years ago, the New Stone (Neolithic) Age began, and with it the first modern revolution. Animals and plants were domesticated, and that meant the nomadic lifestyle came to a gradual end. Middle eastern settlements such as Jericho were founded some 9,000 years ago. For the first time in our history, tradesmen, craftsmen, farmers, herders, merchants, priests, and, inevitably, rulers—then as now almost always strong-men—gathered in urban centers. Commerce between these cities sprang up, and so did war; if you had some grain stored against a bad harvest, unwelcome, hungry, armed, determined, and fierce visitors were a certainty.

Organization on a large scale suddenly became necessary in order to regulate people living in close proximity. We know that organized religion was very important also and played a significant social role. In other words, life became more complex. Military service, property rights, and laws governing daily life became necessary for the first time in our history. Even if they hadn't, no doubt some strongman would have used laws and religion to legitimize his rule.

For 4,000 years, all this took place solely through word of mouth. Imagine sending verbal orders to a distant battlefield and hoping that the memory of the messenger, as well as his loyalty under torture, was unimpeachable. Well, as the old proverb insists, "Necessity is the mother of invention." Of course, writing did not appear in the form in which I am now writing. The first writing was in the form of **ideographs**, symbols that represent ideas. **Pictographs** are pictures that represent ideas and things. **Hieroglyphs** are a form of pictographs peculiar to Egypt. **Syllabic writing**, as you may guess, uses one symbol to represent one syllable. **Alphabetic writing**, such as English, uses one symbol to represent one sound.

Writing is 5,000 years old, however, the first alphabet did not appear until 3,500 years ago, in what today is Lebanon. Its invention propelled civilization in the eastern Mediterranean forward at a very rapid pace. It is interesting that at about the same time, also in the Middle East, the first musical notation appeared.

The first people to communicate by writing were the people of Mesopotamia, or modern-day Iraq, and the Egyptians. More than 4,000 years ago, a people called the Harappans, who have since vanished, began to write in the Indus Valley in what is now Pakistan. About the same time, writing appeared on the island of Crete with the Minoan civilization, which then exported this new skill to Greece. Also at about that time, 2,000 to 1,500 BC, southwestern Iran (then known as Elam), Turkey (then known as the kingdom of the Hittites), and China all began to write.

A relative latecomer to writing was a small island nation called Britannia. Its Roman conquerors brought Latin to its shores 2,100 years ago. However, the inhabitants of Britannia resolutely refused to be civilized, and when the Romans finally left after almost 500 years of trying, the natives promptly forgot their Latin. Soon after the Romans left, the Angles and Saxons and the Danes and Jutes invaded from northern Europe. They swept the indigenous Celts, who spoke an Indo-European language, into the extremities of the islands, now known as Scotland, Wales, Ireland, and Cornwall. Anglo-Saxon and Danish words were appended to the remnants of Celtic and Latin. Five hundred years later, the Normans invaded in 1066 and brought the French language with them, which added and changed many words to the nation's language. After 1564, a man called Shakespeare further enhanced the language by adding hundreds and hundreds of words, many with Greek and Latin roots.

So, as you can see, English as we know it is a mongrel language. George Bernard Shaw pointed out that it is also a strange one. Shaw said that the word "Fish" could just as easily be written as "Ghoti." When asked to prove it, Shaw replied that if you took the "gh" as it is pronounced in the word laugh, the "o" as it is pronounced in the word women and the "ti" as it is pronounced in the word nation, then you could pronounce "ghoti" as fish.

This imprecision is just one of the many obstacles for those who speak English as a second language. A non-English speaker looking at an advertisement that says "Rolaids spells relief" may well rub his eyes, but the richness of the English language is more of an opportunity for communication than a barrier to it.

Despite all this, English is the mother tongue of more than half a billion people and a solid second language to about 400 million more. I have **discovered** that about one quarter of the world speaks an Indo-European-Anglo-Saxon-Danish-Latin-Greek-French hybrid language. I have used this mongrel language to **disclose and share** that fact with you.

Did you know that there are more than 6,000 spoken languages in the world? Did you also know that by the time today's twelfth-grade students are retiring, over half of those languages will have become extinct and mostly replaced by English? Is this good news or bad? Use *Thinking Around the Box*^{TM} before you answer this question!

REASONS TO WRITE ESSAYS

I hope that I have clearly demonstrated in this book how to write an essay. Of course, this information will not be of much use if you do not *practice* writing essays. It probably seems as obvious to you as it is to me that learning the essentials of piano playing from a book is a good first step toward actually being able to play the instrument. It is equally obvious that theoretical knowledge about almost anything, especially piano playing or flying a plane, is not enough; you need to put that knowledge into practice.

One thing is certain, in the future, your writing skills will be on display hundreds of times as you support your application for a job, write a report, or respond to a business letter or e-mail inquiry. Your written words will stand in your stead; whether that is good news or bad news is up to you. Very few people who learn to play the piano will ever depend on that skill to earn a living or to help in some major way with their lives or the lives of members of their families. On the other hand, almost everybody will use writing to earn a living or to help themselves or family members deal with life in civilized society. The benefits of learning how to be a skilled writer have been stated throughout this book. Take a moment to read the list below and you will begin to see them not just as benefits, but also as vital and enduring life skills.

- Essay writing connects reading and writing and gives both a purpose.
- Essay writing improves other skills such as debating or arguing a point and reasoning your way through evidence to a point of view. You can prove a point to yourself by proving it to others.
- Essay writing improves your communication skills.
- Essay writing improves your critical thinking skills.
- Essay writing improves your creative thinking skills.
- Essay writing improves your cognitive (knowledge acquisition) skills.
- Essay writing strengthens the discipline with which you go about acquiring knowledge.
- Essay writing reinforces your belief system and helps you know yourself.
- Essay writing encourages and rewards research by giving it a purpose.

- Essay writing helps you get into college. That is good because the salary gap between high school graduates and college graduates is now 85%, according to the Bureau of Labor Statistics.
- Finally, writing is its own reward. It gives pleasure to its creator.

After reading the above 11 benefits, ask yourself a simple question. What does this mean to me? Now answer your own question. If your answer does *not* prompt you to go back to the beginning of the book and plunge back into the study and practice of the art of essay writing, then I have a quote for you: "If you think education is expensive, try ignorance."

SAMPLE TOPICS

By now, you should be quite familiar with *Thinking Around the Box*™. You know how to discover your point of view on a topic and how to disclose your point of view to others. Here are some topics, or prompts, to help you do the one thing that will now make all the difference in your level of skill—practice:

1. What is the value of art to society?

2. "All truth is not to be told at all times." Do you agree with this?

3. Is it ethical to buy an essay and pass it off as your own work?

4. Discuss the influence of advertising on your life.

5. If your doctor told you that you had only a few months to live, how would you live the rest of your life?

6. Name a modern day hero or heroine, and explain why you consider that person worthy of the title.

7. What causes young people to run away from home?

8. Should all able-bodied citizens be required to perform military service?

9. Many people's public image is different from their private view of themselves. Discuss.

10. Is illegal downloading of music from the Internet immoral, or can it be justified?

11. Should sex education be taught using public funds?

12. Describe one cause for which you would risk your life.

13. Are sports overemphasized in our society?

14. Was it a mistake to give the vote to 18-year-olds?

15. If you could have a conversation with any famous person, living or dead, who would it be, and why?

16. What should we do about crime?

17. What practical measures would you suggest for conserving our wilderness areas?

18. Does portraying violence in the media contribute to violence in society?

19. Explain your reasons for admiring a particular high school teacher.

20. Which has the greatest effect on us—heredity or environment?

21. Which invention or discovery has brought the most long-lasting changes to our civilization?

22. If you had the power to change an historic event such as a war or an election, which would you choose, and why?

23. What characteristics do you look for in a friend?

24. How important is it to know the "right" people in getting ahead in society?

25. What job or career would you absolutely refuse and why?

26. Should people who are paid from public funds have the right to strike?

27. Are professional entertainers and sports figures overpaid?

28. Which of your five senses (sight, touch, smell, taste, or hearing) would you miss most?

29. Should prisoners and welfare recipients be forced to work?

30. Should all the courses that university students take be directly related to their potential careers?

31. Choose a profession and discuss the benefits that society derives from it.

32. Should female soldiers be assigned to combat duties?

33. Attack or defend the practice of advertising, by doctors and lawyers.

34. If you were the programming director of a major TV network, what changes would you make, and why?

35. In what period of history, other than the present, would you like to live and why?

36. More people are living longer in Europe and much of the Americas than in the rest of the world. What effects is that going to have?

37. Why did you choose the career path for which you are preparing?

38. Would you ever reveal a secret entrusted to you by a friend? Why or why not?

39. Would you like to serve in a public office, and why or why not?

40. What rights are humans entitled to, and why?

41. Should it be mandatory for American students to become proficient in a language other than English?

42. Do you or your family support public television and radio, and why or why not?

43. What will you have accomplished in the next 10 years?

44. Should physical education be more rigorous in high school?

45. If you could ban anything in the world, what would it be, and why?

46. Should society emphasize education or punishment for prisoners?

47. Do you have what it takes to be a good parent?

48. What was the most important event in the last decade, and why?

49. Is it better for a political leader to be feared or loved?

50. Courteous behavior belongs to a bygone era and is no longer relevant. Discuss.

51. Nuclear power is the only way to provide energy in the future. Attack or defend.

52. In the USA, we waste a great resource—the elderly. Discuss.

53. Too many of our small children are growing up in day care. Attack or defend.

54. Self-discipline is the most important ingredient for success. Discuss.

55. Does our public education system provide what students need? Discuss.

56. If you could pass one law, what would it be, and why?

57. If you could repeal one law, what would it be, and why?

58. The average American watches 6 hours of TV per day. What are the ramifications of this?

59. Should the teenage children of a divorce choose which parent to live with?

60. Who is the wisest person you have ever heard of, and what made that person wise?

61. What steps would you take to improve the quality of public education?

62. Which of the four seasons appeals to you most, and why?

63. Should every holder of a driver's license have to sign up for the organ donor program?

64. Should "Developed Nations" support less fortunate nations with financial and humanitarian aid only as long as the recipients support the donor's policies?

65. Should all students be obliged to take courses in public speaking?

66. How would you reduce the incidence of intoxicated driving?

67. If you did not have a TV, how would you occupy the time you normally spent watching it?

68. If you were alone on a desert island with plenty of food and water, and sufficient shelter, what books would you want, and why?

69. Should the high school year be extended, and the number of hours that high school students spend in class be increased in order to graduate?

70. What is your view on charitable contributions?

71. Do you read a newspaper every day? If you do, why? If not, why not?

72. Many people consult astrology charts—do you? If so, why?

73. The U.S. Supreme Court has said that it is legal to search a student's property and person for drugs and guns, if there is a reasonable suspicion. Right or wrong?

74. What is your view on immigration, legal or illegal, into the USA?

75. Do Americans place too much emphasis on physical appearance?

76. If you had to choose between a job that you would love and that paid $25,000, and one that paid twice as much, but which you knew you would hate, which would you choose?

77. With the widespread availability of calculators, why is it important to learn arithmetic?

78. Should Americans continue to explore space?

79. Should Americans explore space using manned or unmanned vehicles?

80. Should Americans continue the expensive exploration of the subatomic world of particles?

81. What motivates you?

82. Which forms of entertainment do you find least appealing, and why?

83. Do you like surprises? Explain why or why not.

84. If you did not live in the USA, where would you most like to live and why?

85. Describe some of your family's traditions.

86. Write a review of a movie that you recently saw.

87. Many Americans are overweight and many are too thin. What is happening?

88. Cosmetic surgery. Discuss the pros and cons.

89. The game of checkers.

90. Should we conduct medical research on animals?

91. How important are looks in life?

92. Homelessness in America is at an all-time high. What can be done?

93. Why are talk shows on radio and television so popular?

94. What is the worst kind of injustice?

95. Why do many crimes go unreported?

96. Should doctors be banned from assisting in a suicide?

97. If you could donate $1,000 to a charity, which one would you choose and why?

98. Should convicted felons be allowed to run for public office?

99. Should English be the only language used in American classrooms?

100. Education comes from the Latin word "educare," which means to draw out. The Greeks and Romans believed we are born with knowledge and the teacher's role is simply to draw out that knowledge. Defend or attack this proposition.

A WORD TO THE WISE

If you take nothing else away after reading this book, please remember this: Discovering just who you are is *the* necessary first step towards a personal philosophy, which is the basis for a fulfilling life. Thinking about yourself—not as a selfish exercise, but as a way forward to a meaningful life—is a worthwhile enterprise. Believe me, introspection and self-expression will help with the turbulence and difficult choices that will certainly accompany your progress through life. It will help shape you as you adapt to change, which anyone who has lived longer than you will confirm is the only constant in life. By setting out to discover anything, you are discovering something about yourself also. Before deciding what you want to be, it helps to discover who you are; and writing is the way to do that.

Humans are uniquely gifted; we can reflect on who we are, and we can imagine; the sad truth is that very few of us do. We can ask such questions as "What do I know? What don't I know? What if . . .?" Answering these questions truthfully reveals our authentic self to ourselves, which makes sharing ourselves with others so much more authentic and rewarding.

I have tried to show that writing is without doubt the very best way toward self-discovery. And disclosure, in the form of writing, helps others know who you are. Writing not only gives reading a purpose, as Montaigne said, it helps give a purpose to thinking and living. Your image is reflected in your writing just as surely as it is in a mirror. If the subject you wish to become acquainted with is *you*, then you can only become an expert on the subject with practice, and that means writing.

1. "If you wish to become acquainted with a subject, write . . . about it." (British Prime Minister Benjamin Disraeli)

2. The true subject of an essay is the writer, not the topic being written about.

3. If the true subject matter of an essay is the author, then writing essays must be the best way to discover oneself.

4. It is possible to learn to think one's way to the *discovery* of a personal point of view using disciplined, logical, and structured methods.

5. It is possible to learn to *disclose,* or share, that point of view through clear, concise writing.

6. Practice, practice, practice.

Thoughtful writing is transformational. It leads to better, more informed decision making; not just about essay topics, but about all the decisions that you will make in your life. One final thought: When I was a young student, we had to write answers to all kinds of questions in the form of an essay. It didn't matter whether it was a geometry problem or a discussion of a poem or book we had read. What was interesting, in looking back, is that we were required to put the following initials at the end of the essay: Q E D. These are the initials of the Latin phrase "Quod erat demonstrandum," which in English means "Thus it is proved." In other words, I told you—my reader—what I was going to prove, and then I proved it.

Good luck and best wishes in your career and in your life and remember: **First, use *Thinking Around the Box*^{TM}**.

—Alexander Terego

Winning Essays

These are the three winning essays; all of them attained identical scores, so they are listed alphabetically. I chose them because they all began with a well-thought-out thesis statement that included the thoughts that would be part of their body paragraphs. All three students included their diagrams and freewriting notes. I also awarded marks for the rigor with which the writers followed the seeds sown in the first paragraph, as well as for originality, creativity, authenticity, and an overall sense of their having thought the essay through *before* beginning to write.

All of the students who participated had first read this book. All of them were written by hand in a specified period of time and without reference to other materials. In other words, the essays were composed under SAT/ACT Assessment test-taking conditions. The essays were all written in late October 2004.

essay

What motivates me?

Motivation is something not all of us have. In my case, I am lucky enough to have internal and external motivating forces. I am motivated to be a better person by certain people in my life. I am forever grateful to them for bestowing on me the gift of motivation.

Family is first and foremost. My mother holds me up to a higher standard by expecting the best from me. She leads by example. The niceness that surrounds her is uncanny, and I hope one day to be comparable to her. She motivates me by treating me with respect and understanding.

Friends are a key motivation for me too. The friends I have—even though there are only three—also expect the best from me. This encourages me. I would not be able to live with myself if I knew I had ever let any of them down. Their wit keeps me sharp, and the debates we have encourage me to keep informed about the world around me.

The greatest ardor in my life comes, however, from an unexpected place; it comes from within. I hold myself to a higher standard because others cannot expect me to be something I am not. To clarify, if my friends and family want me to be a leader of a group, it would be merely an empty hope unless I feel the passion to lead. So, the greatest internal motivation is due to the fact that I do not want to let anyone down who believes in me.

The derivatives from which my motivation comes are all different, yet intertwined. Friends and family make my internal motivation much greater. Expectations from myself, however, are my best motivator.

Kate Atkinson, grade 12
Booker High School
Sarasota, Florida

essay

What motivates me?

Generally speaking, I am motivated to do anything by one of two ways: either I see something I have done badly and wish to do better, or I see something I have done well, realize I am capable of doing better, and try to improve. This applies to almost everything in life, not only concrete items like school work and art work, but even abstract things such as relationships or just myself.

This past semester, I was in a class where all the tests were multiple-choice. All my life, I have been terrible at spotting the correct letter, even if I understand the material. Naturally, I did horribly on the first three tests of the semester. When the fourth test rolled around, I reflected on how badly I had done and decided to take charge. I studied harder and practiced multiple-choice tests. For the first time, I actually got a good grade. After that, I realized that it was possible for me to do well on multiple-choice tests. That motivated me to continue; bad grades had motivated me.

This story shows how I can be motivated by both ends of the spectrum. Seeing I have done badly and seeing I have done well motivate me in the same way. This also applies to the way I treat others as well as myself. When I realize that I have treated someone in a way I shouldn't have, it motivates me to want to be a better person. Treating someone better makes me feel better and makes me want to maintain this.

Both of these methods of motivation derive from wishing to improve myself, because of how I acted or performed. The feeling of unfairness I get when I try but don't accomplish what I intended makes me try harder. The great feeling of accomplishment convinces me that I am capable of achieving whatever I wish, which in turn motivates me to try to be even better.

Ilene Godofsky, grade 12
Booker High School
Sarasota, Florida

essay

What would you do if you found out you had three months to live?

"Sir, you have about three months to live." These are words that, if spoken to me, would change the way I would live. I would want to feel as if I had been fulfilled in my life to the fullest. For me to do this, I would have to spend time with my family and travel around the world with friends. I would also love to go skydiving. These are a few things I have always had a desire to do.

Nothing in this world is more precious than family. With only three months to live, I can't think of a better way to spend it than with my family. Family has always been important to me and being with them would make me feel I had filled a gap in myself. I would include not only my parents and siblings, but cousins as well. We could all spend time talking about the good old days, and I could leave them on a happy note.

Almost as important as families are friends. That is why I would like to take a long trip with my friends. I know that, with them, anywhere we went would be the most fun I've ever had; and that's what I would need. I would get to choose, and we would go to some exotic location, somewhere that they would never go for the rest of their lives. My friends are extremely important, and it would be vital for me to get away from everything and take a trip with them all.

I would need a big rush of adrenaline before I died. This would make me feel I had lived life to the fullest. That is why I would go skydiving. The rush and excitement would make me feel that I had done all I could to make my life the best experience I could have—to live like I was dying.

As you can see, with such a short span of time, I would live the remainder of my life to the fullest and make my heart full of good memories. I hope that I would also live in people's memories and hearts, and for the right reasons—I would have made my peace with them.

Marc Kochno, grade 12
Lakewood Ranch High School
Manatee County, Florida

Confusing Word List

abbreviate means *to shorten by omitting*
abridge means *to shorten by condensing*
New York is *abbreviated* to NY.
In order to save time in the reading, the report was *abridged*.

accept means to *receive* or to *agree* to something
except means to *exclude* or *excluding*
I'll *accept* the gift from you.
Everyone *except* my uncle went home.
My uncle was *excepted* from the group of losers.

advantage means *a superior position*
benefit means a *favor conferred or earned* (as a profit)
He had an *advantage* in experience over his opponent.
The rules were changed for his *benefit*.

advice means *counsel* (noun), opinion
advise means *to offer advice* (verb)
Let me give you some free *advice*.
I'd *advise* you to see your doctor.

affect means to *influence* (verb)
effect means to *cause* or *bring about* (verb) or a *result* (noun)
The pollution *affected* our health.
Our lawsuit *effected* a change in the law.
The *effect* of the storm could not be measured.

aggravate means *to make worse*
annoy means *to bother or to irritate*
> Your nasty comments *aggravated* a bad situation.
> Your nasty comments *annoyed* him. (not Your nasty comments aggravated him.)

ain't is an unacceptable contraction for *am not*, *are not*, or *is not*, although *ain't* is sometimes heard in very informal speech

allot means *to give* or *apportion*
> I will *allot* 3 hours for painting the table.
alot is a misspelling of *a lot*
> He earned *a lot* of money. (Better: He earned *a great deal* of money.)

all ready means *everybody* or *everything ready*
already means *previously*
> They were *all ready* to write when the test began.
> They had *already* written the letter.

alright is now often employed in common usage to mean *all right* (In formal usage *all right* is still preferred by most authorities.)
all right means *satisfactory, very well, uninjured,* or *without doubt*
> I'm *alright*, thank you.
> It was his responsibility, *all right*.

all together means *everybody* or *everything together*
altogether means *completely*
> The boys and girls stood *all together* in line.
> His action was *altogether* strange for a person of his type.

almost means *nearly, not quite*
most refers to the *greatest amount or number* or to the *largest part,* a majority
> We are *almost* finished writing the book.
> *Most* of the credit should be given to his uncle.

alongside of means *side by side with*
alongside means *parallel to the side*
> He stood *alongside of* her at the corner.
> Park the car *alongside* the curb.

among is used to discuss *more than two* items

between is used to discuss *two* items only

> The work was divided *among* the four brothers.
>
> She divided the pie *between* Joe and Marie.

amount is used to refer to *a quantity not individually countable*

number is used to refer to *items that can be counted individually*

> A tremendous *amount* of work had piled up on my desk.
>
> We ate a great *number* of cookies at the party.

anxious means *worried*

eager means *keenly desirous*

> We were *anxious* about our first airplane flight.
>
> I am *eager* to see you again.

anyways is an incorrect form for *anyway*

anywheres is an incorrect form for *anywhere*

> I didn't want to go *anyway*.
>
> I couldn't locate her *anywhere*.

aren't I is used informally, but in formal usage *am I not* is correct

> *Am I not* entitled to an explanation?

around should not be used in formal writing as a substitute for *about* or *near*

> I'll be there *about* (not *around*) 2 p.m.

as is not always as clear as *because, for,* or *since* (also see *like*)

> She wants to cry *because* she is very sad.

as used as a *conjunction*, is followed by a verb

like used as a *preposition*, is *not* followed by a verb

> Do as I do, not *as* I say.
>
> Try not to behave *like* a child.

as . . . as is used in an *affirmative* statement

so . . . as is used in a *negative* statement

> She is *as* talented *as* any other actress in the show.
>
> He is *not so* reliable *as* his older brother.

as good as is used for *comparisons*, not to mean *practically*

This bicycle is *as good as* the other one.

They *practically* promised us a place in the hall. (not They *as good as* promised us a place in the hall.)

astonish means *to strike with sudden wonder*
surprise means *to catch unaware*

The extreme violence of the hurricane *astonished* everybody.

A heat wave in April would *surprise us*.

at should be avoided when it does not contribute to the meaning of an idea
Where do you live at? may be heard in informal usage, but *Where do you live?* is the correct form.

The group will arrive *about* noon. (not *at about* noon)

awfully is sometimes heard in informal usage. In formal usage, *very* is correct.

This pie is very good. (not *awfully* good)

a while is used after a preposition (noun)
awhile is used in other cases (adverb)

I coached the team for *a while*.

I coached the team *awhile*.

bad is used after verbs that refer to the senses, such as *look, feel* (adjective)
badly means *greatly, in a bad manner* (adverb)

He felt *bad* that he could not attend the meeting.

The young man needs a part-time job very *badly*.

being as and *being that* should not be used in standard English. *Because* and since are preferable.

Since it was dark, we turned on the lights.

Because he is my friend, I give him a gift.

beside means *at the side of*
besides means *in addition to*

In our tennis game, he played *beside* me at the net.

We entertained Jim, Sue, and Louise, *besides* the members of the chorus.

better means *recovering*
well means *completely recovered*
better is used with the verb *had* to show desirability
> He is *better* now than he was a week ago.
> In a few *more* weeks, he will be *well*.
> He *had better* (not *he better*) follow instructions or pay the penalty.

both means *two considered together*
each means *one of two or more*
> *Both* of the applicants qualified for the position.
> *Each* applicant was given a good reference.

bring means *to carry toward the speaker*
take means *to carry away from the speaker*
> *Bring* the coat to me.
> *Take* money for carfare when you leave.

but that is sometimes heard in informal usage, but in formal usage *that* is correct
> He never doubted *that* she would visit him.

can means *able*
may implies *permission* or *possibility*
> I *can* eat both desserts.
> *May I eat both desserts?*
> It *may* snow tonight.

cannot seem is sometimes used informally, but in formal usage *seems unable* is correct
> My elderly uncle *seems unable* to remember his own phone number.

consistently means *in harmony*
constantly means *regularly, steadily*
> If you give me advice, you should act *consistently* with that advice.
> I *constantly* warned him about leaving the door unlocked.

continual means *happening again and again at short intervals*
continuous means *without interruption*
> The teacher gave the class *continual* warnings.
> Noah experienced *continuous* rain for forty days.

couple refers to *two*, *several* or *a few* refers to more than two

Alex and Frieda are the most graceful couple on the dance floor.

A *few* of my cousinsùMary, Margie, Alice, and Barbaraùwill be at the reunion tonight.

desert (DEZZ-ert) means an *arid area*
desert (di-ZERT) means *to abandon*, or *a reward or punishment* (usually plural)
dessert (di-ZERT) means the *final course of a meal*

I have seen several movies set in the Sahara *desert*.

The soldier was warned not to *desert* his company.

We're certain that execution is a just *desert* for his crime. He received his just *deserts*.

We had strawberry shortcake for *dessert*.

did is the past tense of *do*
done is the past participle of *do*

I *did* whatever was required to complete the job.

I have *done* what you requested.

different than is often used informally, but in formal usage *different from* is correct

Jack is *different from* his brother.

disinterested means *impartial*
uninterested means *not interested*

The judge must be a *disinterested* party in a trial.

I'm an *uninterested* bystander, so I find the proceedings boring.

due to is sometimes used informally at the beginning of a sentence, but in formal usage *because of, on account of*, or some similar expression is preferred

Because of (not due to) the rain, the game was postponed. (BUT: The postponement was *due to* the rain.)

each other refers to *two persons*
one another refers to *more than two persons*

Jane and Jessica have known *each other* for many years.

Several of the girls have known *one another* for many years.

either . . . or is used to refer to choices
neither . . . nor is the negative form
> *Either* Lou *or* Jim will drive you home.
> *Neither* Alice *nor* Carol will be home tonight.

else than is sometimes heard in informal usage, but in formal usage *other than* is correct
> Shakespeare was rarely regarded by students as anything *other than* the writer of plays.

equally as good is an incorrect form; *equally good* or *just as good* is correct
> This bicycle is *just as good* as that one.

everyone, written as one word, is a *pronoun*
every one, written as two words, is used to refer to each *individual*
> *Everyone* present voted for the proposal.
> *Every one* of the voters accepted the proposal.

every bit is incorrect usage for *just as*
> You are *just as* (not *every bit as*) clever as she is.

ever so often means frequently or repeatedly
every so often means *occasionally* or *now and again*
> He sees his brother *ever so often*, practically every day.
> Since tickets are so expensive, we only attend the theater *every so often*.

expect is sometimes used incorrectly to mean *assume* or *presume*
> I *assume* (not *expect*) that he won the race.

fewer is used to refer to items that can be counted
less is used to refer to something viewed as a mass, not as a series of individual items
> I made *fewer* repairs on the new car than on the old one.
> After the scandal, the company enjoyed *less* prestige than it had the previous year.

former means *the first of two*
latter means *the second of two*
> The *former* half of the story was in prose.
> The *latter* half of the story was in poetry.

good is an adjective; *good* is often used informally as an adverb, but the correct word is *well*

> She is a *good* singer.
> She sings *well*.

graduated is followed by the preposition *from* when it indicates completion of a course of study
graduated also means *divided into categories or marked intervals*

> He *graduated from* high school last year. (OR He *was graduated from* high school last year.)
> A *graduated* test tube is one that has marking on it to indicate divisions.

guess is sometimes used informally to mean *think* or *suppose*, but it is incorrect in formal use

> I *think* (not *guess*) I'll go home now.

habit means an *individual tendency to repeat a thing*
custom means *group habit*

> He had a *habit* of breaking glasses before each recital.
> The *custom* of the country was to betroth girls at an early age.

hanged is used in references to a *person*
hung is used in reference to a *thing*

> The prisoner was *hanged* in the town square.
> The drapes were *hung* unevenly.

have got is incorrect usage; *got* should be omitted

> I *have* an umbrella.

healthful is used to express whatever *gives* health
healthy is used to express whatever *has* health

> He follows a *healthful* diet.
> He is a *healthy* person.

hisself is a misspelling of *himself*

> Let him do it *himself*.

humans is used informally to refer to human being, but in formal usage
human beings is correct
> He says that love is a basic need of all *human beings*. (BUT: used as an
> adjective: He says that love is a basic *human* need.)

if introduces a *condition*
whether introduces a *choice*
> I shall go to Greece *if* I win the prize.
> He asked me *whether* I intended to go to Greece.

if it was implies that *something might have been true in the past*
if it were implies *doubt* or indicates *something that is contrary to fact*
> If your book *was* there last night, it is there now.
> *If it were* summer now, we would all go swimming.

imply means *to suggest* or *hint* at (the speaker *implies*)
infer means *to deduce* or *conclude* (the listener infers)
> Are you *implying* that I have disobeyed orders?
> From your carefree tone, what else are we *to infer*?

in is used to indicate *inclusion, location,* or *motion within limits*
into is used for *motion toward* one place *from* another
> The spoons are *in* the drawer.
> We were walking *in* the room.
> I put the spoons *into* the drawer.

in back of means *behind*
in the back of (or *at the back of*) means *in the rear of*
> The shovel is *in back of* (behind) the barn.
> John is sitting *in the back of* the theater.

in regards to is an incorrect form for *in regard to*
> He called me *in regard* to your letter.

instance where is sometimes used informally, but the correct term is *instance
in which*
> Can you tell me of one *instance in which* such a terrible thing occurred?

irregardless in an incorrect form for *regardless*

> I'll be your friend *regardless* of what people say, even if the people are accurate.

is when and *is where* are sometimes used informally, but in formal usage *occurs when* and *is a place where* are correct

> The best scene *occurs when* the audience least expects it.
>
> My favorite vacation spot *is a place where* there are no telephones.

it's is the contraction of *it is* or *it has*
its is a possessive pronoun meaning *belonging to it*

> *It's* a very difficult assignment.
>
> *It is* a very difficult assignment.
>
> We tried to analyze *its* meaning.

kind of and *sort of* are informal expressions that should be rephrased in formal writing—for instance, *somewhat* or *rather* are preferable

> I am *rather* sorry he retired.
>
> He was *somewhat* late for the meeting.

kid is used informally to mean *child* (noun) or *to make fun of* (verb), but is incorrect in formal usage

> My cousin is a very sweet *child*.
>
> They always laugh when you *make fun of* me.

lay means *to put*
lie means *to recline*

> *To lay:*
>
> (present)
>
>> I lay
>
> (past)
>
>> I laid the gift on the table.
>
> (present perfect)
>
>> I have laid
>
> *To lie:*
>
> (present)
>
>> I lie

(past)

I lay on my blanket at the beach.

(present perfect)

I have lain

learn means *to acquire knowledge*
teach means *to give knowledge*

We can *learn* many things just by observing carefully.

He is one actor who likes *to teach* his craft to others.

least means the *smallest in degree* or *lowest rank*
less means the *smaller* or *lower of two*

This is the *least* desirable of all the apartments we have seen.

This apartment is *less* spacious than the one we saw yesterday.

leave means *to go away from* (a verb is NOT used with *leave*)
let means *to permit* (a verb IS used with *let*)

Leave this house at once.

Let me remain in peace in my own house.

lend is a verb meaning to *give to*
loan is a noun denoting *what is given*
borrow means to *take from*

The bank was willing to *lend* him $500.

He was granted a *loan* of $500.

I'd like to *borrow* your electric drill for an hour.

lets is third person singular present of *let*
let's is a contraction for *let us*

He *lets* me park my car in his garage.

Let's go home early today.

libel is a *written and published statement injurious* to a person's character
slander is a *spoken statement of the same sort*

The unsubstantiated negative comments about me in your book constitute *libel*.

When you say these vicious things about me, you are committing *slander*.

like is a preposition used to introduce a phrase
as if is used to introduce a clause (a subject and a verb)
as is a conjunction used to introduce a clause
like if is an incorrect form for *like, as,* or *as if*
> It seems *like* a sunny day.
> It seems *as if* it is going to be a sunny day.
> He acted *as* he was expected to act.

loose means *not fastened or restrained,* or *not tight-fitting*
lose means to *mislay, to be unable to keep, to be defeated*
> The dog got *loose* from the leash.
> Try not *to lose* your umbrella.

many refers to a *number*
much refers to a *quantity* or *amount*
> How *many* inches of rain fell last night?
> *Much* rain fell last night.

may of is an incorrect form for *may have*
might of is an incorrect form for *might have*
> He *may have* been there, but I didn't see him.
> I *might have* gone to the party if I hadn't been ill.
> Note: Contractions of these terms are unacceptable in formal usage.

maybe means *perhaps, possibly* (adverb)
may be shows *possibility* (verb)
> *Maybe* he will meet us later.
> He *may be* here later.

must of is incorrect form for *must have*
> I must have been sleeping when you called. (A contraction of this term is unacceptable in formal usage.)

myself is used as an *intensifier* if the subject of the verb is *I*
myself instead of *I or me,* is not correct
> Since I know *myself* better, let me try it my way.
> My daughter and I (not *myself*) will play.
> They gave my son and *me* (not *myself*) some food.

nice is used informally to mean pleasing, good, fine, but a more exact, less overused word is preferred

This is *sunny* (or *good* or *fine*) weather (not *nice* weather).

He is a *good* (or *kind*) person.

nowheres is incorrect usage for *nowhere*

The dog was *nowhere* to be found.

off of is sometimes used informally, but *off* is correct in formal usage

Joe was taken *off of* the team. (Better: Joe was taken *off* the team.)

on account of is an incorrect form for *because*

We could not meet you *because* we did not receive your message in time.

oral means *spoken*

verbal means *expressed in words*, either spoken or written

Instead of writing a note, she gave him an *oral* message.

Shorthand must usually be transcribed into *verbal* form.

outdoor is an adjective

outdoors is an adverb

We spent the summer at an *outdoor* music camp.

We played string quartets *outdoors*.

owing to is used informally, but in formal usage *because* is preferred

Because of a change of management, his company canceled the takeover attempt.

passed is the past tense of *to pass*

past means just preceding or *an earlier time*

The week *passed* very quickly.

The *past* week was a very exciting one.

people comprise a *united or collective group of individuals*

persons are *individuals that are separate and unrelated*

The *people* of our city will vote for a new bond issue next week.

Only ten *persons* remained in the theater after the first act.

plan on is used informally, but in formal usage *plan to* is correct

Do you *plan to go* (not *plan on going*) to the lecture?

plenty means *abundance* (noun)
plenty is incorrect as an adverb or adjective
> There is *plenty* of room in that compact car.
> That compact car is *very* large (not *plenty* large).

principal means *chief* or *main* (adjective), or a *leader*, or a *sum of money* (noun)
principle means a *fundamental truth or belief*
> His *principal* support comes from the real estate industry.
> The *principal* of the school called a meeting of the faculty.
> He earned 10% interest on the *principal* he invested last year.
> As a matter of *principle*, he refused to register for the draft.

put in is incorrect for to *spend, make,* or *devote*
> Every good student should *spend* (not *put in*) several hours a day doing homework.
> Be sure *to make* (not *put in*) an appearance at the meeting.

quiet means *silent, still*
quit means *to give up or discontinue*
quite means *very or exactly, to the greatest extent*
> My brother is very shy and *quiet*.
> I *quit* the team last week.
> His analysis is *quite* correct.

raise means *to lift, to erect*
raze means *to tear down*
rise means *to get up, to move from a lower to a higher position, to increase in value*
> The neighbors helped him *raise* a new barn.
> The demolition crew *razed* the old building.
> The price of silver will *rise* again this month.

read where is heard in informal usage, but in formal usage *read that* is correct
> I *read that* the troops were being reviewed today.

real is sometimes used informally instead of *really* or *very*, but in formal usage *really* is correct
> He's a *real* good ballplayer. (preferred: He's a *very* good ballplayer.)
> He plays *real* well with the band. (preferred: He plays *really* well with the band.)

reason is because is used informally in speech, but in formal usage *the reason is that* is correct

> The *reason* she calls *is that* (not *because*) she is lonely. (OR She calls *because* she is lonely.)

repeat again is redundant; *again* should be omitted

> Please *repeat* the instructions.

run is used informally to mean *conduct, manage*, but in formal usage *conduct* or a similar word is preferred

> He wants *to conduct* (not *run*) the operation on a profitable basis.

said is sometimes used in business or law to mean *the* or *this*; in formal usage, *the* or *this* is correct

said is also used incorrectly to mean *told someone*

> When *the* (not *said*) coat was returned, it was badly torn.
> The professor *told us* (not *said*) to study for the examination.

same as is an incorrect form for *in the same way as* or *just as*

> The owner's son was treated *in the same way as* any other worker.

says is present tense of *say*

said is past tense of *say*

> He *says* what he means.
> He *said* what he meant. (*Goes* or *went* should not be used instead of *says* or *said*.)

seem is used in informal speech and writing in the expressions *I couldn't seem to* and *I don't seem to*, but in formal usage:

> We *can't find* the address. (not We *can't seem to find* the address.)

set means *to place something down* (mainly)

sit means *to seat oneself* (mainly)

> *To set*:
> (present)
>   He sets
> (past)
>   He set the lamp on the table.
> (present perfect)
>   He has set

To sit:
(present)
  He sits
(past)
  He sat on the chair.
(present perfect)
  He has sat

shall is used with *I and we* in formal usage; informally, I *will* (*would*) may be used

will is used with *you, he, she, it, they*; when an emphatic statement is intended, the rule is reversed
  I *shall* be there today.
  We *shall* pay the rent tomorrow.
  I certainly *will* be there.
  They *shall* not pass.

shape is incorrect when used to mean *state* or *condition*
  The refugees were in *serious condition* (not *shape*) when they arrived here.

should of is an incorrect form for *should have*, which can be contracted to *should've* in speech or informal writing
  You *should've* returned that sweater. (Better: You *should have* returned that sweater.)

sink down is sometimes heard in informal usage, but *down* is redundant and should be omitted
  You can *sink* into the mud if you are not careful.

some time means *a segment of time*
sometime means *at an indefinite time in the future*
sometimes means *occasionally*
  I'll need *some time* to make a decision.
  Let's meet *sometime* next week.
  Sometimes I have an urge to watch a late movie on television.

stationary means *standing still*
stationery means *writing material*
  In ancient times, people thought that the earth was *stationary*.
  We bought our school supplies at the *stationery* store.

suppose means to *assume* or *guess*

supposed is the *past tense* and also *past participle* of *suppose*

supposed also means *ought to* or *should* (when followed by *to*)

> I *suppose* you will be home early.
> I *supposed* you would be home early.
> I had *supposed* you would be there.
> I am *supposed* to be in school tomorrow.

sure is used informally to mean *surely* or *certainly*, but in formal usage *surely* or *certainly* are preferred

> She *sure* is pretty! (Better: She *certainly* is pretty!)
> We will *surely* be in trouble unless we get home soon.

testimony means *information given orally*

evidence means *information given orally or in writing*; *an object* which is presented as proof

> He gave *testimony* to the grand jury.
> He presented written *evidence* to the judge.

than is used to express *comparison*

then is used to express *time* or *a result or consequence*

> Jim ate more *than* we could put on the large plate.
> I knocked on the door, and *then* I entered.
> If you go, *then* I will go too.

than any is used informally in a comparison, but in formal usage *than any other* is preferred

> He is smarter *than any other* boy in the class.

their means *belonging* to them

there means *in that place*

they're is the contraction for *they are*

> We took *their* books home with us.
> Your books are over *there* on the desk.
> *They're* coming over for dinner.

them is the objective case of *they*; it is not used instead of those (the plural of *that*) before a noun

> Give me *those* (not *them*) books!

though means *although* or *as if*

thought is the past tense of *to think*, or *an idea* (noun)

through means *in one side and out another*, *by way of*, *finished*

> *Though* he is my friend, I can't recommend him for this job.
>
> I *thought* you were serious!
>
> We enjoyed running *through* the snow.

to means *in the direction of* (preposition); it is also used before a verb to indicate the *infinitive*

too means *very*, *also*

two is the numeral 2

> We shall go *to* school.
>
> We shall go, *too*.
>
> It is *too* hot today.
>
> I ate *two* sandwiches for lunch.

try and is sometimes used informally instead of *try to*, but in formal usage *try to* is correct

> My acting teacher is going to *try to* attend the opening of my play.

unbeknownst to is unacceptable for *without the knowledge of*

> The young couple decided to get married *without the knowledge of* (not *unbeknownst to*) their parents.

upwards of is an incorrect form for *more than*

> There are *more than* (not *upwards of*) sixty thousand people at the football game.

use means to employ, put into service

used is the past tense and the past participle of use

> I want to use your chair.
>
> I used your chair.

used meaning *in the habit of* or *accustomed to*, is followed by *to*

used is an adjective meaning *not new*

> I am *used* to your comments.
>
> I bought a *used* car.

valuable means *of great worth*
valued means *held in high regard*
invaluable means *priceless*
>This is a *valuable* manuscript.
>You are a *valued* friend.
>A good name is an *invaluable* possession.

weather refers to *atmospheric conditions*
whether introduces a *choice*; it should not be preceded by *of* or *as to*
>I don't like the *weather* in San Francisco.
>He inquired *whether* we were going to the dance.

were is a past tense of *be*
we're is a contraction of *we are*
where refers *to place or location*
>They *were* there yesterday.
>*We're* in charge of the decorations.
>*Where* are we meeting your brother?

which is sometimes used incorrectly to refer to people; it refers to things
who is used to refer to people
that is used to refer to people or things
>He finally returned the books, *which* he had borrowed.
>I am looking for the girl *who* made the call.
>He finally returned the books *that* he had borrowed.
>I am looking for the girl *that* made the call.

while is unacceptable for *and*, *but*, *whereas*, or *though*
>The library is situated on the south side, *whereas* (not *while*) the laboratory is on the north side.
>*Though* (not *while*) I disagree with you, I shall not interfere with your right to express your opinion.

who's is the contraction for *who is* (or who has)
whose means *of whom*, implying ownership
>*Who's* the next batter?
>*Whose* notebook is on the desk?

who is, *who am*—Note these constructions:
    It is *I who am* the most experienced.
    It is *he* who *is* . . .
    It is *he or I who am* . . .
    It is *I or he* who *is* . . .
    It is *he and I who are* . . .

who, *whom*—To determine whether to use *who* or *whom* (without grammar rules):
    (*Who, Whom*) do you think should represent our company?
    Step 1:
        Change the *who—whom* part of the sentence to its natural order:
        Do you think (*who, whom*) should represent our company?
    Step 2:
        Substitute he for *who*, and *him* for *whom*:
        Do you think (*he, him*) should represent our company?
    Step 3:
        Since *he* would be used in this case, the correct form is:
        Who do you think should represent our company?

whoever, *whomever* (see *who, whom* above)
    Give the chair to *whoever* wants it (subject of verb *wants*).
    Speak to *whomever* you see (object of preposition *to*).

win—you *win* a game
beat—you *beat* another player
    We *won* the contest.
    We *beat* (not *won*) the other team.
    (*Beat* is incorrect usage for swindle: The hustler *swindled* the gambler
        out of twenty dollars.)

without is incorrect usage for *unless*
    You will not receive the tickets *unless* (not *without*) you pay for them in
        advance.

your is a possessive, showing ownership
you're is a contraction for *you are*
    Please give him *your* notebook.
    You're very sweet.